INVESTIGATIONS 3

IN NUMBER, DATA, AND SPACE®

STUDENT ACTIVITY BOOK

TERC

PEARSON

Glenview, Illinois • Boston, Massachusetts • Chandler, Arizona • New York, New York

The Investigations curriculum was developed by TERC, Cambridge, MA.

This material is based on work supported by the National Science Foundation ("NSF") under Grant No. ESI-0095450. Any opinions, findings, and conclusions or recommendations expressed in this material are those of the author(s) and do not necessarily reflect the views of the National Science Foundation.

PEARSON

ISBN-13: 978-0-328-86031-9
ISBN-10: 0-328-86031-X

7   18

UNIT 1 Arrays, Factors, and Multiplicative Comparison

UNIT 1 CONTENTS (continued)

UNIT 2 Generating and Representing Measurement Data

UNIT 3 Multiple Towers and Cluster Problems

INVESTIGATION 1

CONTENTS

INVESTIGATION 3

UNIT 4 Measuring and Classifying Shapes

INVESTIGATION 1

UNIT 4 CONTENTS (*continued*)

INVESTIGATION 3

CONTENTS

UNIT 5 Large Numbers and Landmarks

INVESTIGATION 2

UNIT 6 Fraction Cards and Decimal Grids

INVESTIGATION 1

UNIT 6 CONTENTS (*continued*)

INVESTIGATION 3

INVESTIGATION 4

UNIT 6 CONTENTS (continued)

UNIT 7 How Many Packages and Groups?

INVESTIGATION 1

UNIT 8 Penny Jars and Towers

INVESTIGATION 1

Arrays, Factors, and Multiplicative Comparison

Arrays, Factors, and
Multiplicative Comparison

NAME

DATE

How Many in This Array?

This case is completely full of cans.
How many cans are in the case,
including those under the cap? _____

How did you figure this out?

NAME _____ DATE _____

Things That Come in Arrays

Think of things that come in arrays. For each thing you think of, fill in all four columns of the chart.

What Is It?	How Many in the Array?	Dimensions	Drawing of the Array

NAME

DATE

Arrays All Around Us

Item	Total	Dimensions	Array(s)
1	16	2 by 8 8 by 2	
2			
3			
4			

Ongoing Review

5 How many cups of yogurt are there?

Ⓐ 4

Ⓑ 6

Ⓒ 24

Ⓓ 36

NOTE

Students identify the dimensions of rectangular arrays and find the total number in each.

MWI Representing Multiplication with Arrays

© Pearson Education 4

NAME

DATE

More Things That Come in Arrays

Find things at home that come in arrays. For each thing you find, fill in all four columns of the chart.

What Is It?	How Many in the Array?	Dimensions	Drawing of the Array

NOTE

Students are learning about arrays (rectangular arrangements of rows and columns) to help them understand multiplication. Help your child find arrays at home, such as the panes of glass in a window or a six-pack of cans (2 rows of 3).

MWI **Representing Multiplication with Arrays**

NAME   DATE

About the Mathematics in This Unit

Dear Family,

Our class is starting a new mathematics unit about multiplication. In this unit, students review multiplication facts and solve problems by using arrays, such as the examples below. They also solve problems about factors of a number and number relationships, such as this one: If 25 is a factor of 100, will 25 also be a factor of 300? How do you know? Students are introduced to multiplicative comparison problems.

Throughout the unit, students will be working toward these goals:

Benchmarks/Goals	Examples
Use multiplication to solve multiplicative comparison problems.	Franco's daughter is 2 feet tall. Franco is 3 times as tall as his daughter. How tall is he? $3 \times 2 = ?$
Determine whether numbers up to 100 are prime or composite.	Is 49 prime or composite? How do you know? It is composite because $1 \times 49 = 49$ and $7 \times 7 = 49$ so 49 has more than 2 factors.

About the Mathematics in This Unit

Benchmarks/Goals	Examples
Find factors of numbers up to 100 and recognize multiples of single-digit numbers.	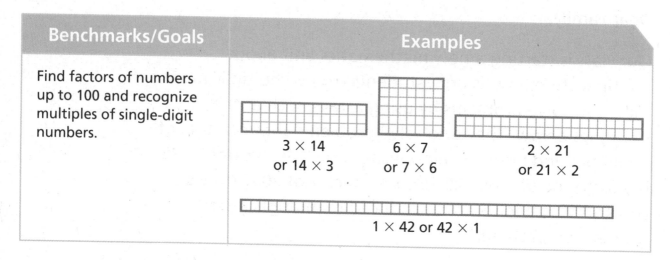

Students will work on multiplication and division in two other Grade 4 units later this year. In these units, they solve problems with larger numbers and share a variety of solution strategies.

In our math class, students spend time discussing problems in depth and are asked to share their reasoning and solutions. It is most important that children accurately and efficiently solve math problems in ways that make sense to them. At home, encourage your child to explain his or her math thinking to you.

Please look for more information and activities that will be sent home in the coming weeks.

NAME _____ DATE _____

Addition Starter Problems

Solve each problem in two different ways, using the first steps given. Show your work clearly.

1 $254 + 763 =$ _____ **a.** Start by solving $200 + 700$.	**b.** Start by solving $250 + 750$.
2 $627 + 575 =$ _____ **a.** Start by solving $600 + 575$.	**b.** Start by solving $27 + 75$.

Ongoing Review

3 Find the missing number: 160, 260, 360, 460, _____

Ⓐ 860   Ⓑ 560   Ⓒ 500   Ⓓ 480

NOTE

Students practice strategies for addition. They work on efficiency and flexibility by solving the same problem in two different ways.

 Addition Strategies

NAME

DATE

Related Activities to Try at Home

Dear Family,

The activities below are related to the mathematics in the unit **Arrays, Factors, and Multiplicative Comparison.** You can use these activities to enrich your child's mathematical learning experiences.

Array Search Look for items around your house or at the grocery store that are packaged or arranged in rectangular arrays: tiles on the floor, eggs in a carton, window panes, a six-pack of juice cans, and so on. Talk with your child about the dimensions (number of rows and columns), and discuss ways to figure out the total number of items.

Arranging Chairs Suppose you have 40 chairs. You want to arrange them into straight rows for an audience to watch a play. You need to arrange the chairs so that there will be the same number in every row. How many different ways could you do this? (What if you start with 50 chairs? 75? 72? 71?)

Modeling Multiplication Situations Encourage your child to help you solve multiplication situations that come up in your daily activities. While you shop, you might ask: How many juice boxes will we have if they come in packages of 3 and we buy 6 packages? At the park, you might ask: If there are 8 soccer teams in our town and each team has 11 players, how many kids play soccer?

NAME   DATE

Looking at Our Arrays

As you walk around and look at our class arrays,
answer the following questions:

1 Which numbers have only one possible array?

2 Which numbers have a square array?

3 Which numbers have the most arrays?

NAME

DATE

How Many Groups?

Complete the following.

1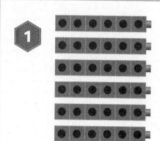

_____ groups of 6 make 36.

_____ $\times\ 6 = 36$

2

_____ groups of 8 make 56.

_____ $\times\ 8 = 56$

3

_____ groups of 7 make 28.

_____ $\times\ 7 = 28$

4

_____ groups of 11 make 33.

_____ $\times\ 11 = 33$

Ongoing Review

5 How many apples are in this crate?

Ⓐ 5

Ⓑ 8

Ⓒ 20

Ⓓ 40

NOTE

Students review multiplication facts as they find missing factors.
MWI Representing Multiplication with Arrays

NAME   DATE

Reviewing Multiplication Facts

Write the answers to these multiplication facts.
Circle any that you do not know immediately.

2 × 2 =	8 × 1 =	2 × 5 =
5 × 10 =	10 × 3 =	3 × 2 =
1 × 7 =	2 × 4 =	5 × 3 =
10 × 8 =	5 × 2 =	2 × 6 =
2 × 7 =	10 × 4 =	8 × 5 =
4 × 5 =	2 × 8 =	9 × 10 =
6 × 10 =	2 × 9 =	6 × 5 =
5 × 7 =	2 × 10 =	5 × 5 =
5 × 9 =	10 × 10 =	7 × 5 =
8 × 2 =	9 × 5 =	7 × 10 =

NOTE

Students practice multiplication facts.

About Mathematics Homework

Dear Family,

Homework is an important link between learning inside and outside school. Homework assignments provide reinforcement of the work students do in math class. Here are some suggestions for making the homework experience successful for your child:

○ Set a regular time every day for homework, and establish a quiet place for your child to work (whether at home, in an after-school program, or at some other place).

○ Establish a system for bringing homework back and forth from school. Use an assignment book, a homework folder, or other organizational tools.

○ Students will bring home the materials and directions needed to do homework activities. Certain materials will be used again and again throughout the year. Because these materials will be sent home only once, please help your child find a safe place to store them—maybe in a math folder or envelope—so that your child can easily locate them when needed. If your child regularly does homework in more than one place, please let me know so we can talk about how to obtain the necessary materials.

○ In our math class, students explore problems in depth and share their reasoning and solutions. It is most important that children accurately and efficiently solve math problems by using problem-solving methods that are meaningful to them. At home, encourage your child to explain his or her strategies and mathematical ideas to you.

About Mathematics Homework

When your child asks you for help in solving a problem, it may be helpful for you to ask questions such as these:

○ What is the problem asking you to figure out?
○ Does this remind you of other problems?
○ What part of the problem do you already know how to solve?
○ What is a good place to start?
○ What have you figured out so far?
○ Would drawing a picture or diagram help?
○ How can I help you (without telling you an answer)?

If you would like to share any thoughts with me about how your child is approaching a homework task, please send me a note. If an assignment seems too difficult, too confusing, or perhaps too easy, let me know so that I can address the issue. I look forward to working with you throughout the year.

NAME   DATE

Array Picture Problems

Problem A

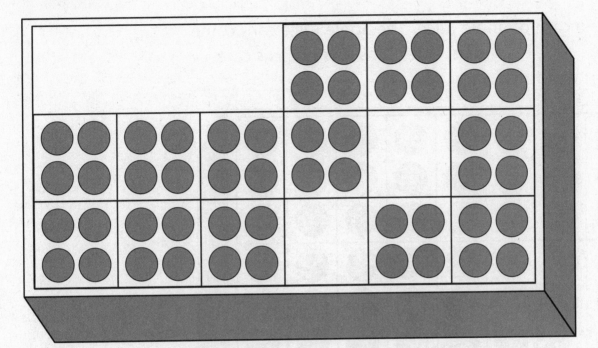

Here is a case of yogurt cups. The yogurt cups come in packs of 4. How many cups of yogurt were in this case when it was full?

How did you figure this out?

Array Picture Problems

Problem B

Here is a case of apple juice. The apple juice cans come in packs of 3. How many juice cans were in this case when it was full?

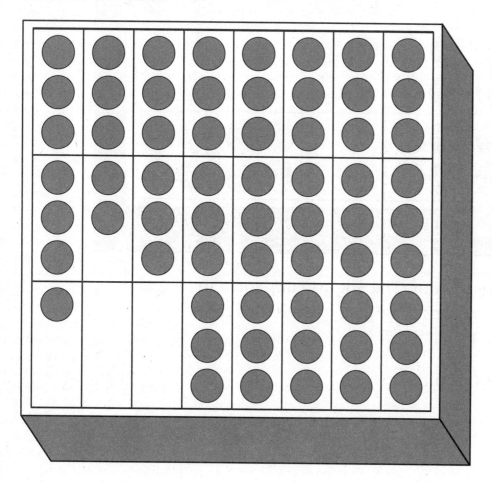

_____ juice cans

Explain how you found your answer.

Array Picture Problems

Problem C

This case is full of apples, but the clipboard is hiding some of them. How many apples are in the case?

_____ apples

Explain how you found your answer.

NAME _____   DATE _____

Class Collections

Solve these problems. Be sure to write the equations that
show how you got your answers.

 1

  a. The students in Ms. Chin's class are collecting bottle caps. They
set a goal of collecting 400 bottle caps. This chart shows how
many bottle caps they collected each week.

Week 1	Week 2	Week 3	Week 4
18	57	62	35

  How many bottle caps did they collect by the end
of 4 weeks?

  b. How many more bottle caps do they need to collect to
reach 400?

2

  a. Mr. Ruiz's class wants to collect 500 rocks for a science project.
Students have brought in these numbers of rocks: 65, 38, and 29.
How many rocks have they collected so far?

  b. How many more rocks do they need to collect to
reach 500?

NOTE

Students solve multi-step problems involving addition and subtraction.

NAME   DATE

Reviewing Multiplication Facts 2

Write the answers to these multiplication facts.
Circle any that you do not know immediately.

$5 \times 3 =$	$2 \times 10 =$	$6 \times 4 =$
$9 \times 5 =$	$7 \times 7 =$	$8 \times 1 =$
$3 \times 8 =$	$2 \times 9 =$	$4 \times 4 =$
$7 \times 6 =$	$5 \times 7 =$	$4 \times 3 =$
$8 \times 5 =$	$5 \times 6 =$	$6 \times 9 =$
$10 \times 10 =$	$4 \times 7 =$	$7 \times 10 =$
$8 \times 9 =$	$3 \times 3 =$	$3 \times 9 =$
$8 \times 6 =$	$1 \times 4 =$	$2 \times 2 =$
$7 \times 2 =$	$6 \times 2 =$	$9 \times 9 =$
$5 \times 10 =$	$2 \times 8 =$	$1 \times 1 =$

NOTE

Students practice multiplication facts.

Multiplicative Comparison Problems

Draw a representation or use cubes to show your thinking about each problem. Write an equation. Be ready to explain how your picture and your equation match the situation. Use additional paper as needed to show your work.

1 Anna picked 6 apples. Sabrina picked 7 times as many apples. How many apples did Sabrina pick?

2 Jake's grandmother lives 8 miles away from him. His aunt lives 6 times as far away from him as his grandmother. How far away does his aunt live?

3 In a zoo there is an eastern diamondback rattlesnake that is 6 feet long, and a reticulated python that is 4 times as long as the rattlesnake. How many feet long is the python?

© Pearson Education **4**

Multiplicative Comparison Problems

4 Marisol has 12 stamps in her stamp collection. Cheyenne has 3 times as many stamps. How many stamps does Cheyenne have?

5 Amelia has 24 marbles. She has 6 times as many marbles as Steve. How many marbles does Steve have?

6 Tonya's farm is 9 acres. Emaan's farm has 4 times as many acres. How many acres is Emaan's farm?

NAME

DATE

Solving Multiplicative Comparison Problems

Solve each problem and show how you solved it.
Write an equation for each problem.

1 Over the summer Noemi read 9 books.
Sei read 4 times as many books. How many
books did Sei read?

2 Benson's tomato plant is 3 feet tall. His corn
plant is twice as tall as his tomato plant. How
tall is his corn plant?

3 Luke has lived in Suntown for 6 years. Yuson has
lived in Suntown for 3 times as many years. How
many years has Yuson lived in Suntown?

4 Lake Chelan in Washington State is 55 miles long.
Lake Chelan is 5 times as long as Long Lake in
Maine. How long is Long Lake?

NOTE

Students solve multiplicative comparison problems.

Prime or Composite

Determine whether each number is prime or composite.
Explain how you know.

1   Is 42 prime or composite? How do you know?

2   Is 13 prime or composite? How do you know?

3   Is 57 prime or composite? How do you know?

4   Is 80 prime or composite? How do you know?

5   Is 95 prime or composite? How do you know?

6   Is 29 prime or composite? How do you know?

NAME   DATE

More Multiplicative Comparison Problems

Solve each problem and show how you solved it. Write an equation for each problem. Use additional paper as needed to show your work.

1 Sabrina is 9 years old. Her grandmother is 8 times as old as Sabrina. How old is her grandmother?

2 Helena is 5 feet tall. A tree in Helena's yard is 35 feet tall. The tree is how many times as tall as Helena? Draw a representation or use cubes to show your thinking about this problem. Write an equation. Be ready to explain how your representation and your equation match the situation. Use additional paper as needed to show your work.

3 The library has 6 books about Madrid, Spain. It has 6 times as many books about London, England. How many library books are there about London, England?

4 Andrew picked 7 yellow roses and 28 red roses. How many times as many red roses did Andrew pick than yellow roses?

NAME

DATE

Collecting 1,000 Pennies

Solve these problems. Be sure to write the equations that show how you got your answers.

The students in Ms. Shapiro's class want to collect 1,000 pennies in one month.

1 After the first week, they had collected 267 pennies. How many more do they need to collect to reach 1,000?

2 After two weeks, they had collected a total of 516 pennies. How many more do they now need to reach 1,000?

3 After 3 weeks, they had collected a total of 843 pennies. How many more do they need to collect in the last week to reach 1,000?

NOTE

Students practice making 1,000 in a story problem context.
MWI Subtraction Strategies

NAME _____ DATE _____

More Prime or Composite

Determine whether each number is prime or composite.
Explain how you know.

1 Is 36 prime or composite? How do you know?

2 Is 7 prime or composite? How do you know?

3 Is 21 prime or composite? How do you know?

4 Is 23 prime or composite? How do you know?

5 Is 70 prime or composite? How do you know?

NOTE

Students determine whether numbers are prime or composite.
MWI **Prime and Composite Numbers**

NAME _____ DATE _____

Distance Problems

1 **a.** Elena's family is taking a bicycle vacation over 4 days. They plan to bicycle 115 miles in all. Write an addition equation that shows one possible combination of miles they could bike over 4 days.

_____ + _____ + _____ + _____ = 115

b. Write another equation to show a second way they could bike a total of 115 miles.

_____ + _____ + _____ + _____ = 115

2 **a.** Edwin and his family are driving to a family reunion 516 miles away. They have 3 days to drive the total distance. Write an addition equation that shows one possible combination of miles they could drive over 3 days.

_____ + _____ + _____ = 516

b. Write another equation to show a second way they could drive a total of 516 miles.

_____ + _____ + _____ = 516

Ongoing Review

3 $124 + 127 + 125 =$ _____

Ⓐ 376   Ⓑ 375   Ⓒ 372   Ⓓ 366

NOTE

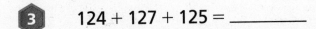

Students practice addition in a story problem context, finding a combination of addends that equals a given sum.

NAME

DATE

Related Problem Sets

Solve the related problems in each set. As you work on these problems, think about how solving the first problem in each set may help you solve the others.

1
500	500	500
− 85	− 185	− 187

2
$400 - 200 =$ _____

$400 - 180 =$ _____

$420 - 180 =$ _____

3
$300 - 150 =$ _____

$350 - 150 =$ _____

$353 - 150 =$ _____

$353 - 147 =$ _____

4
$189 - 55 =$ _____

$189 - 155 =$ _____

$289 - 155 =$ _____

$289 - 165 =$ _____

5
$600 +$ _____ $= 1,000$

$650 +$ _____ $= 1,000$

$655 +$ _____ $= 1,000$

$658 +$ _____ $= 1,000$

6
300	305	299
300	299	296
+ 300	+ 296	+ 290

Ongoing Review

7 Which does NOT equal 404?

Ⓐ $199 + 205$ Ⓑ $201 + 203$ Ⓒ $198 + 202$ Ⓓ $202 + 202$

NOTE

Students solve addition and subtraction problems in related sets.

NAME

DATE

Factors and Products

Fill in the chart with the missing factors or products.

Factor	×	Factor	=	Product
	×	8	=	56
4	×	7	=	
6	×		=	54
	×	5	=	30
3	×	9	=	
7	×		=	49
8	×	6	=	
10	×		=	100
	×	9	=	81

NOTE

Students review multiplication facts by finding products or missing factors.

MWI **Factors**

NAME

DATE

Finding the Factors of 100

Find the factors of 100. You may use the 100 Chart, cubes, arrays, grid paper, or drawings to help you make sure that the numbers you choose are factors. Record the factors in the chart.

Factor	How Many in 100?	Factor Pair
Example: 1	100	100 × 1

When you think you have found all of the factors of 100, list them here.

_____

_____

_____

NAME   DATE

Finding the Factors of 200

Find the factors of 200. Record the factors in the chart. You can use multiplication facts you know to help you. You can also use the 300 Chart, cubes, arrays, grid paper, or drawings to find the factors.

Factor	How Many in 200?	Factor Pair	Factor	How Many in 200?	Factor Pair

When you think you have found all of the factors of 200, list them here.

_____

_____

_____

NAME

DATE

Finding the Factors of 300

Find the factors of 300. Record the factors in the chart. You can use multiplication facts you know to help you. You can also use the 300 Chart, cubes, arrays, grid paper, or drawings to find the factors.

Factor	How Many in 300?	Factor Pair	Factor	How Many in 300?	Factor Pair

When you think you have found all of the factors of 300, list them here.

_____

_____

_____

NAME

DATE

How Many More?

Solve these problems. Show your solutions.

1   621 + _____ = 950

2   481 + _____ = 895

3   508 + _____ = 780

4   437 + _____ = 1,100

NOTE

Students find the missing number to make a correct addition equation.

NAME   DATE

More Factors and Products

Fill in the chart with the missing factors or products.

Factor	×	Factor	=	Product
10	×	9	=	
	×	7	=	28
7	×	8	=	
9	×		=	63
8	×	9	=	
	×	6	=	42
5	×	8	=	
6	×		=	48
4	×		=	36

NOTE

Students review multiplication facts by finding products or missing factors for multiplicative equations.

MWI **Factors**

NAME   DATE

Finding the Factors of Other Multiples of 100

Choose a multiple of 100 that is greater than 300, such as 400, 500, or 600. Write this number in the blanks below, "How Many in _____?" Record the factors of that number in the chart. Use multiplication facts you know to help you. You can also use the 300 chart, cubes, arrays, grid paper, or drawings.

Factor	How Many in ___?	Factor Pair	Factor	How Many in ___?	Factor Pair

When you think you have found all of the factors of this multiple, list them here.

_____

Finding the Factors of Other Multiples of 100

Now choose another multiple of 100 that is greater than 300. Record the factors of that number in the chart. Keep using multiplication facts you know to help you, along with the 300 chart, cubes, arrays, grid paper, or drawings.

Factor	How Many in _____?	Factor Pair	Factor	How Many in _____?	Factor Pair

When you think you have found all of the factors of this multiple, list them here.

_____

NAME

DATE

Story Problems

Solve these problems. Show how you got your answers.

1 Marisa had 574 stamps in her stamp collection. She gave 255 stamps to her brother to start his own collection. Then Marisa's aunt gave her 449 stamps. How many stamps does Marisa have in her collection now?

2 Ms. Gomez is running for the city council. She printed 1,000 campaign brochures for the elections. On the first day, she gave away 387 brochures. On the second day, she gave away 515 brochures. How many brochures does she have left?

3 a. Devon earned $13.50 for babysitting his niece. He also earned $4.50 for doing his chores that week. He wants to buy a backpack that costs $18.45. Does he have enough money?

b. If he does not have enough money, how much more does he need?

NOTE

Students solve multi-step addition and subtraction problems in a story problem context.
MWI Addition Strategies

NAME   DATE

How Many People Counted?

Read the problems, and answer the questions. Explain how you can solve the problems without actually doing the skip counting. What do you know that will help you?

1 Ms. McCoy's class counted by 20s. How many people counted to get to 300? How do you know?

2 Mr. Harris's class counted by 10s. How many people counted to get to 300? How do you know?

3 Ms. Gomez's class counted by 25s. How many people counted to get to 300? How do you know?

NOTE

Students have been finding the multiples of given numbers in a routine called *Counting Around the Class* (for example, 20, 40, 60, 80, . . .). Here, they practice finding a series of multiples of a number.

MWI **Multiples: Counting Around the Class**

NAME   DATE

Factors of 16 and 48

1 Find the factors of 16 and the factors of 48.
Use arrays, pictures, or cubes to show your
thinking.

Factors of 16:

Factors of 48:

Factors of 16 and 48

2 Use a representation (picture, array, cubes) to explain why all of the factors of 16 are also factors of 48.

3 32 and 64 are multiples of 16.

$2 \times 16 = 32$

$4 \times 16 = 64$

Do you think all of the factors of 16 are also factors of 32 and 64? Are the factors of 16 also factors of other multiples of 16? Explain your thinking.

NAME   DATE

More Multiplicative Comparison Problems 2

Solve each problem and show how you solved it.
Write an equation for each problem.

1 Daniela ate 7 raisins for her snack. Jamal ate 3 times as many raisins for his snack. How many raisins did Jamal eat?

2 Gregory's old crayon box has 8 crayons in it. His new crayon box has 32 crayons in it. How many times as many crayons does Gregory's new box have than the old box?

3 There are 9 red notebooks for sale at the store. There are 6 times as many blue notebooks for sale at the store. How many blue notebooks are there?

4 Jake picked 7 strawberries. Sarah picked 35 strawberries. How many times as many strawberries did Sarah pick?

NOTE

Students solve multiplicative comparison problems.
MWI Multiplicative Comparison

NAME

DATE

Multiplying by Factors of 100

Solve each set of problems. Look for patterns that might help you.

1 $2 \times 50 =$ _____

$4 \times 50 =$ _____

$6 \times 50 =$ _____

2 $4 \times 25 =$ _____

$6 \times 25 =$ _____

$8 \times 25 =$ _____

3 _____ $\times 4 = 100$

_____ $\times 4 = 200$

_____ $\times 4 = 300$

4 $10 \times$ _____ $= 200$

$10 \times$ _____ $= 300$

$10 \times$ _____ $= 400$

5 $5 \times 20 =$ _____

$10 \times 20 =$ _____

$15 \times 20 =$ _____

6 _____ $\times 5 = 100$

_____ $\times 5 = 200$

_____ $\times 5 = 400$

NOTE

Students have been finding factors of 100, 200, and 300. Here, they solve multiplication problems that involve these factors.

MWI Multiplication Cluster Problems

NAME

DATE

Rock On!

Solve each problem. Draw the arrays and write equations.
Use another sheet of paper if you need to.

1 Rock bands often stack their speakers in an array. One teen band has 24 speakers. They stack them at least 2 high, but no taller than 8 high. What are all the different arrays they can make?

2 One band has 30 speakers. They stack them at least 3 high, but no taller than 6 high. What are all the different arrays they could make?

3 Another band has 48 speakers. They stack them at least 4 high, but no taller than 6 high. What are all the different arrays they can make?

4 One band has fewer than 40 speakers. They stack them in an array exactly 9 high. How many speakers could they have? Explain how you know.

NOTE

Students find arrays for given numbers with restraints.

MWI Representing Multiplication with Arrays

Generating and Representing Measurement Data

Generating
and Representing
Measurement Data

NAME

DATE

Prime or Composite

Determine whether each number is prime or composite.
Explain how you know.

1 Is 8 prime or composite? How do you know?

2 Is 15 prime or composite? How do you know?

3 Is 47 prime or composite? How do you know?

4 Is 27 prime or composite? How do you know?

5 Is 88 prime or composite? How do you know?

NOTE

Students identify numbers less than 100 as either prime or composite and explain how they know.
MWI **Prime and Composite Numbers**

NAME   DATE

About the Mathematics in This Unit

Dear Families,

Our class is starting a new mathematics unit about modeling with data called *Generating and Representing Measurement Data*. During this unit, students collect, represent, describe, and interpret data.

Throughout the unit, students work toward these goals:

Benchmark/Goals	Examples
Use a line plot to organize, represent, and analyze data about two groups in order to compare the groups.	
Design a data question that involves measurement to compare two groups.	
Use a line plot to represent measurement data that includes fractions.	

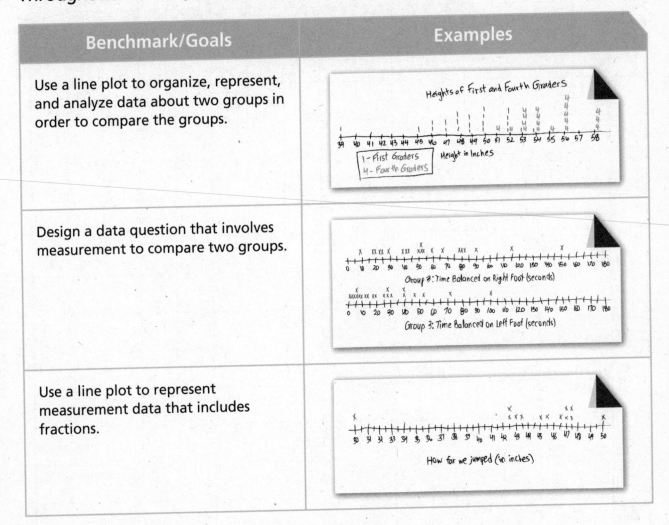

Please look for more information and activities about Unit 2 that will be sent home in the coming week.

NAME _____ DATE _____

Party Supplies

Solve each of the story problems below. Show your thinking.

1 Ms. Ruiz bought 13 packages of cups for a big party. Each package contains 8 cups. How many cups did she buy?

2 Ms. Ruiz bought 9 packages of plates for the party. Each package contains 12 plates. How many plates did she buy?

3 Ms. Ruiz bought 7 packages of napkins for the party. Each package contains 16 napkins. How many napkins did she buy?

Ongoing Review

4 Which product is greater than 70?

Ⓐ 7×9 Ⓒ 5×11

Ⓑ 6×12 Ⓓ 8×8

NOTE

Students practice solving multiplication problems in a story context.
MWI **Representing Multiplication with Arrays**

NAME _____   DATE _____

How Many People Counted?

In these counting problems, each student said one number.

1 The students in Ms. Alonzo's class counted by 20s.
The first student said 20, the second student said 40,
and the third said 60. How many students counted
to get to 300? _____
How do you know?

2 The students in Mr. Nelson's class counted by 15s.
The first student said 15, the second student said 30,
and the third said 45. How many students counted
to get to 300? _____
How do you know?

3 The students in Ms. Weinberg's class counted by 25s.
The first student said 25, the second student said 50,
and the third student said 75.

    a. How many students counted to get to 300? _____
    How do you know?

    b. When the students in Ms. Weinberg's class counted
    by 25s, did anyone say the number 180? _____
    How do you know?

NOTE

Students find the multiples of a given number and solve multiplication problems.
MWI **Multiples: Counting Around the Class**

© Pearson Education 4

NAME _____   DATE _____

Related Activities to Try at Home

Dear Family,

The activities below are related to the mathematics in the data unit, *Generating and Describing Measurement Data*. You can use the activities to enrich your child's mathematical learning experience.

Data in the Media We live in an information-rich society, and it is important for students to begin to experience the variety of ways that information is communicated and represented in the world. As you are reading the newspaper or a magazine, point out various graphs and charts to your child. Talk about how you make sense of the data, what they mean, and why you are interested in them. This is an opportunity for you to show your child how graphs communicate important information to you and your family.

Investigate a Topic You and your child may also be interested in investigating a problem that you have noticed in your community. You might start by defining the problem and devising a plan to collect data about it. As a next step, you could collect the data and then organize and represent the results. As you work, you might think about who is an appropriate audience for your findings.

For example, one household collected data about the number of cars that passed by their house at rush hour compared with other times in the day. They made a series of recommendations to improve traffic safety in their neighborhood and circulated the recommendations to their neighbors and to the police department.

NAME _____ DATE _____

Factors

For each of the following numbers, list as many pairs of factors as you can.

Example: 28 ___2___ × ___14___ ___4___ × ___7___ ___1___ × ___28___	**24** _____ × _____ _____ × _____ _____ × _____ _____ × _____
32 _____ × _____ _____ × _____ _____ × _____	**18** _____ × _____ _____ × _____ _____ × _____
16 _____ × _____ _____ × _____ _____ × _____	**20** _____ × _____ _____ × _____ _____ × _____

NOTE

Students find pairs of factors for a given product.

MWI **Factors**

NAME   DATE

How Many Cavities?

How many cavities have you had?

NOTE

Students are gathering data about the number of cavities they have had for a class data investigation.

MWI **Organizing and Representing Data**

NAME

DATE

Comparing the Heights of Fourth and First Graders

1 How do the heights of the first graders compare with the heights of the fourth graders in your class? Write three statements about this question.

In your statements include ideas about the data such as these: Where are there lots of data? How big are clumps of data? What are the tallest heights and the shortest heights? What outliers are there? What do you think are the typical heights of first graders and of fourth graders?

a. _____

_____

b. _____

_____

c. _____

_____

2 About how much taller do you think a fourth grader is than a first grader? Why do you think so? Support your ideas with evidence from the data.

_____

_____

_____

_____

_____

_____

_____ _____
NAME   DATE

Counting Around the Class

1 Mr. Patel's students counted by 5s. The first person said 5, the second said 10, and the third said 15. Each student said one number. How many students counted to get to 100? _____
How do you know?

2 Ms. Bailey's students counted by 10s. The first person said 10, the second said 20, and the third said 30. Each student said one number.

    a. How many students counted to get to 270? _____
    How do you know?

    b. When Ms. Bailey's students counted by 10s, did anyone say the number 225? _____
    How do you know?

Ongoing Review

3 Which has the same product as 3×12?

    Ⓐ 8×4 Ⓒ 6×6

    Ⓑ 6×24 Ⓓ 9×6

NOTE

Students find the multiples of a given number and solve multiplication problems.
MWI Multiples: Counting Around the Class

NAME

DATE

Things That Come in Groups

Solve the story problems below. Write a multiplication equation for each problem and show how you solved it.

Spiders have 8 legs.

1 How many legs are on 5 spiders? _____

Equation: $\underline{\quad 5 \times 8 = \quad}$ _____

2 How many legs are on 11 spiders? _____

Equation: _____

3 How many legs are on 16 spiders? _____

Equation: _____

Ongoing Review

4 Which is not a factor of 54?

Ⓐ 3   Ⓒ 8

Ⓑ 6   Ⓓ 9

NOTE

Students practice multiplication by solving story problems.
MWI Representing Multiplication with Arrays

NAME

DATE

Arranging Cans of Juice

 a. You have 32 cans of juice. Show all the ways you can arrange these cans into arrays. Draw the arrays on a separate sheet of paper.

b. List all the factors of 32.

2 **a.** Mauricio has 36 cans of juice. Show all the ways he can arrange his cans into arrays. Draw the arrays on a separate sheet of paper.

b. List all the factors of 36.

Ongoing Review

 Which number is prime?

Ⓐ 49 Ⓑ 27 Ⓒ 17 Ⓓ 9

NOTE

Students find factors by drawing rectangular arrays for quantities of objects.
MWI **Factors**

Choosing a Data Question

Answer the following questions to plan your data project.

1 Choose a question that you can answer by collecting measurement data. (Think about an interesting question that results in measuring length, distance, or time.)

_____

_____

_____

_____

2 What two groups will you be comparing?

_____

_____

_____

_____

3 What materials will you need? (What you are going to measure with? Are any other materials needed?)

_____

_____

_____

_____

Choosing a Data Question

4   Explain in detail the procedures you are going to use for your measurement. Think about how you can make your measurements in the same way every time.

_____

_____

_____

_____

_____

_____

5   Try out your question and measurement method. Revise if necessary. Ask three other students your question, and do the necessary measurements. Ask these students if your question makes sense, and consider whether you need to make any changes to your question or your measurement method. If you revise your question or method, write your new question and method here:

_____

_____

_____

_____

_____

_____

Choosing a Data Question

6 Plan how to collect and record your data.

Think about the following:

○ How are you going to record the data as you collect them?
○ What information do you need to write?
○ How are you going to keep track of which people you have asked?
○ Who is going to do what?

Write how you will record and keep track of your data.

_____

_____

_____

_____

_____

_____

_____

NAME _____ DATE _____

Peanut Count

Each of the students in Mr. Herrera's class took a handful of trail mix and counted the number of peanuts.

1 Make a line plot of the data.

Peanut Count					
Benson	8	Steve	8	LaTanya	8
Yuki	5	Damian	8	Marisol	9
Noemi	6	Lucy	8	Andrew	8
Derek	13	Yuson	6	Ursula	10
Bill	10	Anna	7	Sabrina	6
Abdul	9	Helena	9	Richard	6

2 What would you say is the typical number of peanuts in this trail mix? Explain why you think so.

_____

_____

NOTE

Students represent data in a line plot.
MWI **Organizing and Representing Data**

How Many Cubes Can Students Grab?

Students in a third-grade class collected data about how many cubes kindergartners and third graders could grab with one hand. They put their data in two line plots.

Kindergartners
Number of Cubes Grabbed in One Hand

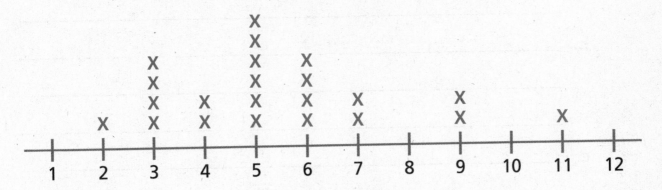

Third Graders
Number of Cubes Grabbed in One Hand

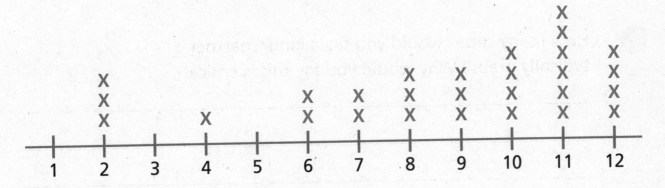

NOTE

In this homework, students look carefully at the shapes of two different sets of data and compare them.

MWI **Describing and Summarizing Data**

© Pearson Education 4

How Many Cubes Can Students Grab?

1 Write three statements about the number of cubes third graders and kindergartners grabbed.

a. _____

_____

_____

b. _____

_____

_____

c. _____

_____

_____

2 How many cubes would you say a kindergartner typically grabs? Why would you say this is typical?

_____

_____

_____

3 How many cubes would you say a third grader typically grabs? Why would you say this is typical?

_____

_____

_____

NAME

DATE

Number of Houses

Ollie counted the number of houses on each block between home and school. The line plot shows Ollie's data.

Number of Houses

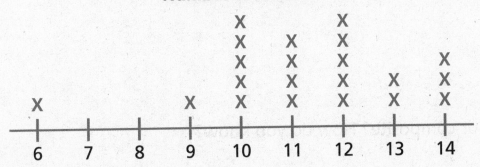

1 What would you say is the typical number of houses per block? Explain why you think so.

_____

_____

_____

_____

2 An *outlier* is a piece of data that "lies outside" the rest of the data. Is there any outlier? If so, what is it and what might account for this unusual piece of data?

_____

_____

_____

_____

NOTE _____

Students describe features of a set of data on a line plot.
MWI **Describing and Summarizing Data**

© Pearson Education 4

Composite or Prime?

Determine whether each number is prime or composite.
Explain how you know.

1   Is 30 prime or composite? How do you know?

2   Is 57 prime or composite? How do you know?

3   Is 79 prime or composite? How do you know?

4   Is 53 prime or composite? How do you know?

5   Is 97 prime or composite? How do you know?

NOTE

Students identify numbers less than 100 as either prime or composite and explain
how they know.
MWI **Prime and Composite Numbers**

Comparison Problems

Solve each problem and show how you solved it. Write an equation for each problem.

1 Kerry sold 8 boxes of cookies. Janet sold 7 times as many boxes. How many boxes did Janet sell?

2 Sue answered 3 questions correctly on the first science test. She answered 15 correctly on the first math test. Sue got _____ times as many math questions correct as she did science questions.

3 There are 6 red pens for sale at the store. There are 4 times as many blue pens for sale at the store. How many blue pens are there?

4 Terrell and Jill were in a play. Terrell said 9 lines. Jill said 81 lines. How many times more lines did Jill say?

NOTE

Students solve multiplicative comparison problems.
MWI **Multiplicative Comparison**

What Did You Learn From Your Data Project?

1 What was your question?

_____

_____

2 Suppose that a teacher was interested in your data question and asked, "What did you learn from your project?" Write at least three things you learned. Give evidence from the data.

_____

_____

_____

_____

_____

_____

_____

© Pearson Education 4

What Did You Learn From Your Data Project?

3 How did your results compare to what you thought they would be? Did anything about your results surprise you?

_____

_____

_____

_____

4 Now that you have learned some things about your question, can you think of some other questions that you would ask to learn more about this topic?

_____

_____

_____

_____

5 What else did you learn about data investigations from doing this project?

_____

_____

_____

_____

NAME

DATE

Leg Riddles

Birds have 2 legs.
Dogs have 4 legs.
Ladybugs have 6 legs.

1 There are 48 legs, and they all belong to dogs. How many dogs are there?

2 There are 3 ladybugs, 7 dogs, and 13 birds in the house. How many legs are there all together?

3 There are 36 legs in the house. All the legs belong to birds, dogs, and ladybugs. How many of each creature— birds, dogs, and ladybugs—might be in the house?

(There are many possible answers. How many can you find?)

Birds	Dogs	Ladybugs

NOTE

Students solve multiplication and division problems in story problem contexts.

NAME _____ DATE _____

Arranging Cans of Juice

Solve the following problems.

 a. You have 28 cans of juice. Show all of the ways you can arrange these cans into arrays. Draw the arrays in the space below.

b. List all of the factors of 28.

NOTE

Students find factors by arranging objects into rectangular arrays.
MWI Representing Multiplication with Arrays

Arranging Cans of Juice

2

a. Mauricio has 42 cans of juice. Show all of the ways he can arrange his cans into arrays. Draw the arrays in the space below.

b. List all of the factors of 42.

NAME   DATE

Mystery Data A

The table and graph below show the same data. These data represent some group of living things.

Individual	Inches	Individual	Inches	Individual	Inches
A	82	I	77	Q	83
B	85	J	84	R	79
C	78	K	72	S	82
D	75	L	79	T	75
E	83	M	75	U	79
F	83	N	80	V	80
G	83	O	84	W	74
H	81	P	76	X	76

Heights or Lengths of Members of a Group of Living Things in Inches

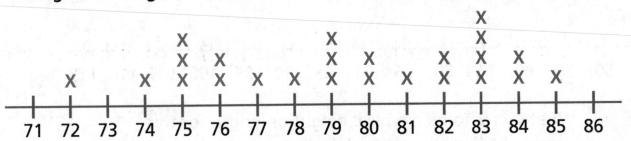

1. What seems to be a typical height or length for this group of living things? Explain why you think so.

_____

_____

2. What do you think the group could be? Give reasons for your answer.

_____

_____

_____

NAME

DATE

Mystery Data B

The table and graph below show the same data. These data represent some group of living things.

Individual	Inches	Individual	Inches	Individual	Inches
A	78	G	86	M	84
B	96	H	93	N	80
C	114	I	64	O	72
D	94	J	54	P	54
E	63	K	72	Q	79
F	72	L	108	R	116

Heights or Lengths of Members of a Group of Living Things in Inches

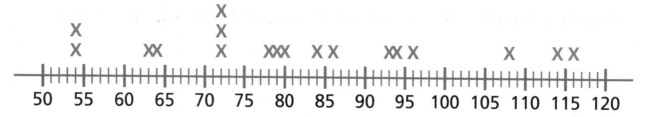

1 What seems to be a typical height or length for this group of living things? Explain why you think so.

_____

_____

2 What do you think the group could be? Give reasons for your answer.

_____

_____

_____

NAME   DATE

Mystery Data C

The data below represent some group of living things.

Individual	Inches	Individual	Inches
A	18.5	P	18
B	19.5	Q	20
C	19	R	20
D	20	S	21
E	19	T	20
F	20	U	20
G	20	V	20
H	18.5	W	19
I	18	X	19
J	21.5	Y	20.5
K	22	Z	19
L	19	AA	19
M	19	BB	19.5
N	19.5	CC	19
O	19	DD	20

Mystery Data C

1 Make a line plot of the heights or lengths of these living things.

Heights or Lengths of Members of a Group of Living Things in Inches

---

2 What seems to be a typical height or length for this group of living things? Explain why you think so.

_____

_____

3 What do you think the group could be? Give reasons for your answer.

_____

_____

_____

_____

Parking Lot Data

The students in Ms. May's class counted the cars in the school parking lot at the beginning of every school day for a month.

1 Represent the data in a line plot.

Number of Cars in the Parking Lot				
18	23	22	25	20
23	19	17	24	23
22	23	25	24	24
22	23	22	24	25

2 Describe the data. Include a discussion of the range, where the data are concentrated or spread out, whether there are any outliers, and what is typical about the data set as a whole

___

___

___

___

NOTE

Students represent and describe a set of data.
MWI Describing and Summarizing Data

NAME   DATE

More Composite or Prime?

Determine whether each number is prime or composite.
Explain how you know.

1 Is 21 prime or composite? How do you know?

2 Is 39 prime or composite? How do you know?

3 Is 55 prime or composite? How do you know?

4 Is 63 prime or composite? How do you know?

5 Is 87 prime or composite? How do you know?

NOTE

Students identify numbers less than 100 as either prime or composite and explain how they know.

MWI **Prime and Composite Numbers**

NAME

DATE

How Heavy Is Your Pumpkin?

1 Organize the data in a line plot.

Pumpkin Weights (in pounds)

12	3	4	10	3
6	$11\frac{1}{2}$	$4\frac{1}{2}$	9	$12\frac{1}{2}$
3	2	$2\frac{1}{2}$	4	
11	$4\frac{1}{2}$	$7\frac{1}{2}$	11	

2 Describe the data. Include a discussion of the range, where the data are concentrated or spread out, whether there are any outliers, and what is typical about the data set as a whole.

_____

_____

_____

_____

_____

Ongoing Review

3 Half of the pumpkins weigh less than

Ⓐ 5 pounds   Ⓑ 4 pounds   Ⓒ 3 pounds   Ⓓ 2 pounds

NOTE

Students practice representing and describing data.
MWI **Describing and Summarizing Data**

Multiple Towers and Cluster Problems

Multiple Towers and
Cluster Problems

NAME   DATE

Mr. Jones and the Bagels

Show how you solve each problem.

 1   Mr. Jones needs to buy 14 dozen bagels for a big party.
(Remember that a dozen is 12.)

    a. Mr. Jones goes to the bagel shop. They only have
10 dozen bagels left! So he buys them all. How many
bagels does he buy at the bagel shop?

    b. Mr. Jones goes to the supermarket to buy the rest of
the bagels. How many more bagels does Mr. Jones need
to buy? Make a picture or diagram that would prove to
someone else how many more he needs to buy.

    c. How many bagels did Mr. Jones buy altogether?

NAME

DATE

Multiplication Story Problems

Show how you solve each problem.

1 Ruth and Manuel are helping Mr. Jones set up for the party. They will need 8 chairs at each table. Ruth sets up 9 tables and Manuel sets up 9 tables. How many chairs do they need altogether?

2 Mr. Jones bought cans of juice, which come in 6-packs. He bought eight 6-packs of orange juice and five 6-packs of apple juice. How many cans of juice did he buy?

3 Mr. Jones realizes that he didn't buy enough juice! He goes back to the store and finds juice boxes that come in 9-packs. He buys ten 9-packs of orange juice and six 9-packs of apple juice. How many juice boxes does he buy? Make a picture or diagram that would prove to someone else how many juice boxes he buys.

NAME   DATE

TV Time

Jan asked her friends how many hours they watched TV on Friday. She wrote down their answers.

$2, 2\frac{1}{2}, 2, 3\frac{1}{2}, 2\frac{1}{2}, 1, 3, 2\frac{1}{2}, 2, 1\frac{1}{2}, 1\frac{1}{2}, 1, \frac{1}{2}, 2$

1   Make a line plot showing these data.

2   What is the difference between the most TV watched and the least TV watched?

Ongoing Review

3   Kevin watched 3 hours of TV last week. Jan watched 5 times as much TV as Kevin. How many hours of TV did Jan watch?

   Ⓐ 2　　　　Ⓑ 8　　　　Ⓒ 9　　　　Ⓓ 15

NOTE

Students make a line plot and answer questions about the data that involve subtraction and multiplication.

MWI **Organizing and Representing Data**

　　　　© Pearson Education 4

NAME   DATE

Planning a Party

Show how you solve each problem.

1 The party store sells cups in packs of 8. Ms. Ruiz wanted 15 packs of cups. She bought 10 packs of blue cups and 5 packs of purple cups. How many blue cups did she buy? How many purple cups did she buy? How many cups did she buy altogether?

2 Ms. Ruiz bought 12 packages of plates for the party. Each package contains 15 plates. She bought 10 packages of small plates and 2 packages of large plates. How many small plates did she buy? How many large plates did she buy? How many plates did she buy altogether?

3 Ms. Ruiz also bought forks and spoons at the store. The forks and spoons come in packs of 9. She bought 10 packages of forks and 7 packages of spoons. How many forks and spoons did she buy altogether?

NOTE

Students practice solving multiplication problems in a story context.

© Pearson Education 4

About the Mathematics in This Unit

Dear Family,

Our class is starting a new unit about multiplication and division called *Multiple Towers and Cluster Problems*. During this unit, students will build on the work they did in Unit 1. Students will be solving multiplication problems with 2-digit numbers, division word problems, and problems about multiples and number relationships.

Throughout the unit, students work toward these goals:

Benchmarks/Goals	Examples
Multiply 2-digit numbers by 1-digit and small 2-digit numbers (e.g., 12, 15, 20) using strategies that involve breaking the numbers apart.	$\begin{array}{r} 37 \\ \times\ 6 \\ \hline \end{array}$ $6 \times 37 = (6 \times 30) + (6 \times 7)$ $6 \times 37 = 180 + 42$ $6 \times 37 = 222$
Solve division problems (2-digit and small 3-digit numbers divided by 1-digit numbers), including some that result in a remainder.	There are 52 people taking a trip. Each van holds 8 people. How many vans do they need? $52 \div 8$ is 6 R4. They need 7 vans.

© Pearson Education 4

About the Mathematics in This Unit

Benchmarks/Goals	Examples
Multiply a number by a multiple of 10.	3×4 3×40 $3 \times 40 = 3 \times 4 \times 10 = 12 \times 10 = 120$

Students will work on multiplication and division again later this year in Unit 7, when they will solve problems with larger numbers and share a variety of solution strategies.

In our math class, students spend time discussing problems in depth and are asked to share their reasoning and solutions. It is most important that children accurately and efficiently solve math problems in ways that make sense to them. At home, encourage your child to explain his or her math thinking to you.

Please look for more information and activities about Unit 3 that will be sent home in the coming weeks.

NAME _____ DATE _____

How Many People Counted?

1 The students in Ms. Zeller's class counted by 3s. Each student said one number. The first student said 3, the second student said 6, the third said 9, and so on.

How many students counted to get to 57? _____

How do you know?

2 The students in Mr. Martinez's class counted by 6s. The first student said 6, the second student said 12, the third student said 18, and so on.

How many students counted to get to 126? _____

How do you know?

3 The students in Ms. Brennan's class counted by 7s. The first student said 7, the second student said 14, the third student said 21, and so on.

a. How many students counted to get to 126? _____

How do you know?

b. When the students in Ms. Brennan's class counted by 7s, did anyone say the number 91? _____

How do you know?

NOTE

Students find the multiples of a given number and solve multiplication problems.

MWI Multiples: Counting Around the Class

NAME   DATE

Leg Riddles

Birds have 2 legs.
Hamsters have 4 legs.
Beetles have 6 legs.

1 There are 52 legs and they all belong to hamsters.
How many hamsters are there?

2 There are 4 beetles, 5 hamsters, and 11 birds in the
house. How many legs are there altogether?

3 There are 32 legs in the house. All the legs belong to birds,
hamsters, and beetles. How many of each creature—birds,
hamsters, and beetles—might be in the house?

There are many possible answers. How many can you
find? Use the table below to show different solutions
to this problem.

Birds	Hamsters	Beetles

NOTE

Students solve multiplication and division problems in story problem contexts.

Arranging Cans of Soup

1 **a.** Amelia has 32 cans of soup. Show all the ways she can arrange these cans into arrays. Draw the arrays in the space below.

 2 **a.** Nikolai has 36 cans of soup. Show all the ways he can arrange his cans into arrays. Draw the arrays in the space below.

b. List all the factors of 32.

b. List all the factors of 36.

Ongoing Review

 3 Which number is prime?

Ⓐ 49   Ⓑ 27   Ⓒ 17   Ⓓ 9

NOTE

Students find factors by arranging numbers into rectangular arrays.

MWI **Factors**

NAME   DATE

Matching Arrays

Complete the multiplication equation illustrated by each set
of arrays.

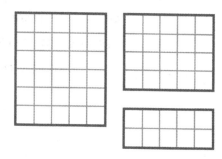

$6 \times 5 = ($ _____ $\times 5) + ($ _____ $\times 5)$

2

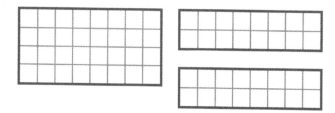

$4 \times$ _____ $= ($ _____ $\times$ _____ $) + ($ _____ $\times$ _____ $)$

3

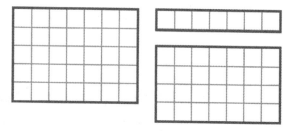

_____ $\times$ _____ $= ($ _____ $\times$ _____ $) + ($ _____ $\times$ _____ $)$

4 Draw an array of your own choosing. Then draw two
more arrays that together match your first array.
Write a multiplication equation for your diagram.

NOTE

Students practice breaking apart multiplication problems to make them easier to solve.
MWI Representing Multiplication with Arrays

NAME

DATE

Related Activities to Try at Home

Dear Family,

The activities described here are related to the mathematics in Unit 3. Use the activities to enrich your child's learning experience.

Modeling Division Situations At school, students are solving word problems that represent various types of division situations. Encourage your child to help you solve situations that come up in your daily activities. Here are some examples: "I baked a batch of 48 cookies for the bake sale. I need to put them into bags of 5. How many bags of 5 can I make? What can I do with the extra cookies?" "There are 180 players who will play baseball in teams of 9. How many teams can they make?"

How Did You Solve That? Ask your child to tell you about how he or she is multiplying and dividing. Show that you are interested in these approaches. Because these strategies may be unfamiliar to you, listen carefully to your child's explanation; you might even try to do a problem or two using the new procedure. Let your child be the teacher!

NAME

DATE

Breaking Up Arrays

1 Two small arrays have been combined to make a big array. What are the dimensions and product of the big array? Fill in the equation that shows how the Big Array equals the combination of the two small arrays.

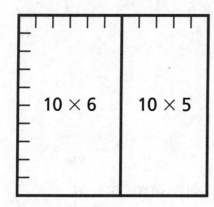

Big Array

Dimensions of the Big Array: _____

Product: _____

Equation: _____ × _____ = (_____ × _____) + (_____ × _____)

2 Draw an array for 12 × 7. (You don't have to draw all the boxes inside, just the shape and the dimensions.) Show how you would break up this array into two smaller arrays. Fill in the equation and solve the problem.

Array:

Equation: _____ × _____ = (_____ × _____) + (_____ × _____)

Product: 12 × 7 = _____

Solving Multiplication Problems

Show how you solve each problem.

1 How many wheels are on 27 cars?

2 One kind of starfish has 5 arms. How many arms are on 21 starfish?

3 Luke has 16 marbles. Jill has 7 times as many marbles. How many marbles does Jill have?

Solving Multiplication Problems

Show your thinking for each problem.

4 $5 \times 19 =$

5 $23 \times 3 =$

6 $6 \times 13 =$

NAME   DATE

Fundraiser Comparisons

Show how you solve each problem.

1 Katie sold 35 bags of popcorn for a fundraiser. She sold 5 times as many as Aaron. How many bags did Aaron sell?

2 Luis sold 12 cans of peanuts for the fundraiser. Mike sold 4 times as many as Luis. How many cans did Mike sell?

3 Lupe sold 39 bags of cheese popcorn. She sold 3 times as many bags as Frances. How many bags did Frances sell?

Ongoing Review

4 Paula has sold $256 worth of items for the fundraiser. She has sold $32 more than Steve. How much has Steve sold?

    Ⓐ $8   Ⓑ $64   Ⓒ $224   Ⓓ $288

NOTE

Students practice solving multiplication problems involving multiplicative comparison.
MWI Multiplicative Comparison

NAME   DATE

Lots of Legs

Show how you solve each problem.

1 How many legs are on 21 spiders? (A spider has 8 legs.)

2 How many legs are on 28 horses?

3 $5 \times 17 =$

4 $24 \times 6 =$

Ongoing Review

5 Which product does **not** equal 100?

Ⓐ 50×2 Ⓑ 4×20 Ⓒ 10×10 Ⓓ 25×4

NOTE

Students practice solving multiplication problems.
MWI **Strategies for Solving Multiplication Problems**

Division Stories

Show how you solve each problem.

1 The 48 fourth graders at the Glendale School are taking a field trip to the science museum. They need to split into groups of 3 students for a special science project at the museum. How many groups will there be?

2 At the science museum gift shop, Michelle, Devon, Teresa, and Omar buy a bag of 64 marbles. They want to divide the marbles equally among the 4 of them. How many marbles will each fourth grader get?

Division Stories

3 Mrs. Santos got a shipment of 84 oranges. She has room for 6 rows of oranges on a table in her window display. How many oranges will be in each row if she puts the same number in each row?

4 Mrs. Santos asks her helper to divide a box of 65 apples into bags of 5 apples each. How many bags can her helper make?

NAME

DATE

More Leg Riddles

People have 2 legs.
Cats have 4 legs.
Spiders have 8 legs.

People	Cats	Spiders

1 There are 3 spiders, 2 cats, and 5 people in the house. How many legs are there altogether?

2 There are 28 legs and they all belong to cats. How many cats are there?

3 There are 30 legs in the house. All of the legs belong to people, cats, and spiders. How many of each creature—people, cats, and spiders—might be in the house?

There are many possible answers. How many can you find? Use the table to show your solutions.

NOTE

Students solve multiplication problems in story problem contexts.

Division Problems

Show how you solve each problem.

1 Yuki and Jake made 52 snowballs. If they wanted to share them evenly with 2 other friends, how many snowballs would each of the 4 of them get?

2 Ramona has saved $63. She has saved 3 times has much money as Luke. How much money has Luke saved?

3 Devon wants to plant 84 tomato plants in his garden. He wants to put 7 plants in each row. How many rows will he need?

NOTE

Students practice solving division problems in a story problem context.
MWI Division Situations

NAME _____   DATE _____

What Do You Do with the Extras?

Solve the division problem. Then solve each story problem. For each problem, decide what to do with the extras and explain your answer. Make drawings for Problems 1, 2, and 4.

44 ÷ 8

Answer: _____

1 There are 44 people taking a trip in some small vans. Each van holds 8 people. How many vans will they need?

Make a drawing for this problem that would explain your answer to someone else.

2 If 8 people share 44 crackers equally, how many crackers does each person get?

Make a drawing for this problem that would explain your answer to someone else.

What Do You Do with the Extras?

3 If 8 people share 44 balloons equally, how many balloons does each person get?

4 There are 44 students going to see a movie. Each row holds 8 people. How many rows do they fill up?

Make a drawing for this problem that would explain your answer to someone else.

5 On Sunday, 8 friends earned $44 by washing people's cars. They want to share the money equally. How much money does each friend get?

NAME _____ DATE _____

Division with Remainders

Solve the division problem. Then solve each story problem.

40 ÷ 3

Answer: _____

1 Three people share 40 crackers evenly. How many crackers does each person get?

2 Three people share 40 pencils evenly. How many pencils does each person get?

3 Forty people are lined up to ride the ski lift to the top of the mountain. Each chair on the lift holds 3 people. How many chairs will it take to get everyone up the mountain in one trip?

Ongoing Review

4 The Dance Club is going on a field trip to the ballet. There are 22 people in the Dance Club. Four people can ride in each car. How many cars will they need?

ⓐ 2 cars ⓑ 4 cars ⓒ 5 cars ⓓ 6 cars

NOTE

Students practice doing division and interpreting remainders in a story problem context.
MWI Remainders: What Do You Do With the Extras?

© Pearson Education 4

NAME   DATE

Story Problems

Solve each problem. Show your work. Write a multiplication
or division equation for each one.

1 Becca is building toy cars. She bought a box of 60 little
wheels to use on the cars. How many cars can she build
with the 60 wheels? Each car has 4 wheels.

2 On Monday, Ms. Wu bought 8 packages of pencils.
Each package contains 6 pencils. On Tuesday, Ms. Wu
went back to the store and bought 4 more packages.
How many pencils did Ms. Wu buy in all?

NOTE

Students practice solving multiplication and division problems in a story problem context.
MWI **Division and Multiplication**

**ACTIVITY**

More Division Stories

Solve these problems and show your thinking. Be sure to make a drawing for Problem 5 that you can use to prove your answer.

1 Cheyenne and her father baked 72 cookies for the school bake sale. They plan to put them in bags of 4 cookies each. How many bags of cookies can they fill?

2 Aliya, Ethan, Brianna, and Will saved up a total of $74 from returning bottles and cans. They want to share it equally among the 4 of them. How much money will each of the friends receive?

3 Juice boxes come in packages of 3. The fourth graders at Glendale School need 125 juice boxes for their field trip. How many packages of juice boxes will they have to buy?

ACTIVITY

More Division Stories

4 The art teacher at Center School bought a box of 80 pencils for the 6 students in her drawing class. How many pencils will each student get if they share the pencils equally?

5 Marisol lives in a house in Orchardville. The tallest building in Orchardville is 115 feet tall. It is 5 times taller than Marisol's house. How tall is Marisol's house?

Make a drawing for this problem that would explain your answer to someone else.

Factor Pairs

For each of these numbers, list as many pairs of factors as you can.

1 36	2 30
Example: 3 × 12	
3 40	4 48
5 60	6 72

Ongoing Review

7 Which of these has the greatest product?

Ⓐ 8 × 7 Ⓑ 9 × 6 Ⓒ 10 × 5 Ⓓ 11 × 4

NOTE

Students practice multiplication by finding pairs of factors for a given product.

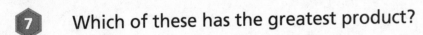 **Factors**

NAME   DATE

How Many People Counted?

Try to solve these problems without doing the skip counting yourself. What do you know that will help you?

1   Mr. Harris's class counted by 25s. Each person said one number. How many people counted to get to 200? How do you know?

2   Ms. Tamura's class also counted by 25s. Each person said one number. How many people counted to get to 400? How do you know?

3   Ms. Gomez's class counted by 20s. Each person said one number. How many people counted to get to 300? How many people have to count to get to 600? How do you know?

NOTE

Students have been working with factors of 100 and multiples of 100 in an activity called *Counting Around the Class*. This page provides practice with these ideas.

MWI **Multiples: Counting Around the Class**

NAME

DATE

Division and Remainders

Solve these problems and explain your answers.

1 There are 70 people in line for the roller coaster. Each car holds 8 people. How many cars will it take for everyone to ride at the same time?

2 Eighty people bought tickets for a boat ride. Twelve people can ride in one boat. How many boats can be completely filled?

3 How many prizes could you get with 100 tickets?

ARCADE PRIZES

6 tickets per prize

4 Mr. Brown's class counted around the class by 5s. The number they ended with was 135. How many students counted?

NOTE

Students practice doing division and interpreting remainders in story problem contexts.

MWI Remainders: **What Do You Do With the Extras?**

© Pearson Education **4**

NAME

DATE

What's the Story?

Write a story for each division problem. Then solve it.

 1 $45 \div 9$

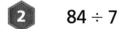 **2** $84 \div 7$

NOTE

Students practice writing and solving division story problems.
MWI Division Situations

Related Multiplication and Division Problems

Solve the problems and show how you solve them. Write a multiplication or division equation for each problem.

 1

a. Mrs. Santos got a new shipment of apples. There were 20 bags of apples in the shipment. Each bag contained 8 apples. How many apples did Mrs. Santos receive?

b. Jeff bought a book with 160 pages. If he reads 8 pages each day, how many days will it take him to finish the book?

c. Could you use the solution to Problem 1a to help you solve Problem 1b? If so, how?

d. Make a drawing that you could use to explain to someone else how you can use Problem 1a to help solve Problem 1b.

Related Multiplication and Division Problems

 a. There are 3 fourth-grade classes at Washington Elementary School. There are 21 students in each class. How many fourth graders are there in all?

b. Jessica and two of her friends earned $63 at a neighborhood car wash. They want to share the money equally among the 3 of them. How much money does each friend get?

c. Could you use the solution to Problem 2a to help you solve Problem 2b? If so, how?

Related Multiplication and Division Problems

a. A scientist was observing a frog that was 5 inches long. It jumped 32 times its body length. How far did the frog jump?

b. Nadeem has 160 bottle caps in his bottle cap collection. He has 32 times more bottle caps in his collection than Benson. How many bottle caps does Benson have in his collection?

c. Could you use the solution to Problem 3a to help you solve Problem 3b? If so, how?

NAME

DATE

Factors and Products

Fill in the chart with the missing factors or products.

Factor	×	Factor	=	Product
10	×	5	=	
10	×		=	150
	×	20	=	100
	×	20	=	200
	×	20	=	300
25	×		=	75
25	×		=	150
25	×		=	300
4	×	25	=	
4	×		=	200
4	×		=	400
	×	10	=	200
	×	20	=	200
	×	25	=	200

NOTE

Students practice solving multiplication problems.

MWI **Factors and Multiples**

NAME

DATE

Simpler Parts

Solve each problem by following the clues.

1 $136 \div 4 =$ _____

How many 4s are in 100? _____

How many 4s are in 36? _____

How many 4s are in 136? _____

2 $104 \div 8 =$ _____

How many 8s are in 80? _____

How many 8s are in 24? _____

How many 8s are in 104? _____

3 $162 \div 6 =$ _____

How many 6s are in 120? _____

How many 6s are in 42? _____

How many 6s are in 162? _____

Ongoing Review

4   Which of these expressions is equal to 6?

    Ⓐ $100 \div 20$ Ⓑ $48 \div 8$ Ⓒ $63 \div 9$ Ⓓ $30 \div 3$

NOTE

Students practice breaking apart division problems into smaller problems.
MWI Division Strategies

About Our Multiple Tower

Answer these questions about the multiple tower that you and your partner built.

1 What number did you use to build your multiple tower? _____

2 What is the ending multiple on your tower? _____

3 How many multiples are in your tower? _____

4 What is one way to figure out how many multiples are in your tower without counting each one?

About Our Multiple Tower

Answer these next questions without counting up on your tower.

5   What is the 10th multiple? _____

6   What is the 20th multiple? _____

7   What is the 25th multiple? _____

8   How did you decide what the 20th multiple is?

9   Find each of the multiples above (10th, 20th, 25th) on your tower, and label them with a multiplication expression such as 10×30.

10   What other landmark multiples can you find and label?

NAME _____ DATE _____

Arranging Juice Cans

1 You have 24 juice cans. Show all of the ways you can arrange these cans into arrays. Draw the arrays on a separate sheet of paper.

2 List all the factors of 24.

3 Teyo has 25 juice cans. Show all of the ways he can arrange his cans into arrays. Draw the arrays on a separate sheet of paper.

4 List all the factors of 25.

5 Karina says, "25 has more factors than 24 because 25 is greater than 24." Do you agree or disagree with Karina? Explain.

NOTE

Students solve story problems that involve finding factors.
MWI **Factors**

NAME   DATE

A Multiple Tower

 a. Make a multiple tower for 13. Write the first 5 multiples of 13.

b. Write an equation that represents the 5th multiple of 13.

c. What will the 10th multiple be in this multiple tower of 13? How do you know?

d. What will the 20th multiple be? How do you know?

e. What will the 25th multiple be? How do you know?

NOTE

Students practice solving multiplication problems using the context of a multiple tower.

MWI Multiple Towers

NAME

DATE

Problems About Oranges

Solve each problem and record your solution with an equation. Make a quick picture or diagram that shows how the two problems are related.

1 Ms. Santos sells bags of oranges in her grocery store. There are 4 oranges in each bag. David bought 6 bags of oranges to bring to his class. How many oranges did David buy?

2 When Ms. Santos orders oranges from the fruit company, they come in boxes. Each box has 40 oranges inside. Last week, Ms. Santos ordered 6 boxes of oranges. How many oranges did she order?

Multiplying by Multiples of 10: What Happens?

Solve these problems.

1 $5 \times 6 =$ _____

$50 \times 6 =$ _____

2 $3 \times 4 =$ _____

$30 \times 4 =$ _____

3 $8 \times 6 =$ _____

$80 \times 6 =$ _____

Multiplying by Multiples of 10: What Happens?

Now answer the following questions.

4 What do you notice about your solutions to the problems on page 132? In each set, how are your answers related?

5 Use a picture or diagram to show your thinking for the problems in Set 1 on page 132.

6 Try solving this problem:

$5 \times 600 =$

How is your answer to this problem different from your answer to 5×60? Why do you think that is?

NAME   DATE

Kayla's Multiple Tower

The picture shows part of Kayla's multiple tower.

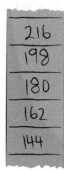

1 What number did Kayla count by? How do you know?

| 216 |
| 198 |
| 180 |
| 162 |
| 144 |

2 How many numbers are in Kayla's tower so far? How do you know?

3 Write a multiplication equation that represents how many numbers are in Kayla's multiple tower.

_____ × _____ = _____

4 What is the 10th multiple in Kayla's tower?

5 Suppose that Kayla adds more multiples to her tower.

a. What will be the 20th multiple in her tower? How do you know?

b. What will be the 25th multiple in her tower? How do you know?

Ongoing Review

6 Which of these numbers is not on Kayla's multiple tower?

Ⓐ 9   Ⓑ 18   Ⓒ 72   Ⓓ 90

NOTE

Students practice solving multiplication and division problems.
MWI **Multiple Towers**

NAME   DATE

Story Problems 2

Solve the story problem. Show your solution with equations.
You may also show your solution with arrays or pictures
of groups.

 Ms. O'Riley, the art teacher, orders crayons that come
in boxes of 40. This year she ordered 9 boxes. How many
crayons did she order?

NOTE

Students practice multiplying by a number that is a multiple of 10 in a story problem context.
MWI **Multiplying Groups of 10**

© Pearson Education 4

NAME   DATE

Story Problems 2

2 Write a story problem to go with the following multiplication expression. Then solve the problem and show your thinking.

7×50

Story Problems About 10s

Solve these problems and show your thinking.

1   Last month Lakewood School ordered 8 boxes of erasers
with 20 erasers in each box. How many erasers did
they order?

2   Every year, Ms. Ortega orders a box of 50 erasers
for each classroom at Riverview School. There are
11 classrooms in the school. How many erasers does
Ms. Ortega order?

3   Last year at Lincoln School, Mr. Johnson ordered 7 boxes
with 120 erasers in each box. How many erasers did
Mr. Johnson order?

Story Problems About 10s

4   Last year Mr. Johnson ordered 70 packs of paper. This year Mr. Johnson order 6 times as many packs of paper.
How many packs of paper did Mr. Johnson order this year?

5   The Lakewood School ordered 80 notebooks for the 4th-grade classes. They ordered 8 times as many boxes of pencils. How many boxes of pencils did they order?

DAILY PRACTICE

NAME _____ DATE _____

Things That Come in Groups

Show how you solve each problem. Write a multiplication equation that shows your answer.

Spiders have 8 legs.

1 How many legs do 6 spiders have? _____

Equation: _____

2 How many legs do 12 spiders have? _____

Equation: _____

3 How many legs do 18 spiders have? _____

Equation: _____

NOTE _____

Students practice multiplication by solving story problems.
MWI Multiple Towers

© Pearson Education 4

NAME

DATE

Multiplying Groups of 10

Solve each pair of multiplication problems.

1 $8 \times 4 =$ _____

$8 \times 40 =$ _____

2 $6 \times 7 =$ _____

$6 \times 70 =$ _____

3 $9 \times 5 =$ _____

$90 \times 5 =$ _____

4 $12 \times 6 =$ _____

$120 \times 6 =$ _____

5 $15 \times 4 =$ _____

$15 \times 40 =$ _____

6 $5 \times 14 =$ _____

$50 \times 14 =$ _____

7 $11 \times 3 =$ _____

$11 \times 30 =$ _____

8 $40 \times 5 =$ _____

$400 \times 5 =$ _____

NOTE

Students are learning how multiplying one number in a multiplication problem by 10 affects the product. Here, they solve problems with numbers that are multiples of 10.

MWI **Multiplying Groups of 10**

NAME

DATE

Ms. Santos's Apples

Solve these problems. Record your solution with equations.
Use pictures or diagrams to show what is happening in
the problem.

1 Ms. Santos has 120 apples. She wants to pack them into
boxes with 20 in each box. How many boxes does
she need?

2 When Ms. Santos started to pack the apples into boxes,
she found that her boxes were too small. She could fit
only 10 apples in each box. Now how many boxes
does she need?

ACTIVITY

Doubles and Halves

1 Solve the first problem in each pair. Can you use the first problem to help you solve the second problem?

a. $8 \times 4 =$ _____

$16 \times 4 =$ _____

b. $8 \times 6 =$ _____

$16 \times 3 =$ _____

c. $16 \times 3 =$ _____

$16 \times 6 =$ _____

d. $9 \times 8 =$ _____

$18 \times 4 =$ _____

e. $18 \times 8 =$ _____

$18 \times 4 =$ _____

f. $15 \times 8 =$ _____

$30 \times 4 =$ _____

NAME   DATE

Doubles and Halves

2   Look at your solutions to the two problems in 1f.

    a. Use arrays, pictures, or a story context to show how
       the two problems are related.

    b. Explain what your representation shows.

    c. Write a rule about what you think happens when
       you double one factor and cut the other factor in
       half in a multiplication problem.

NAME   DATE

Counting Around the Class

Solve these problems.

1   Mr. Bugwadia's class counted by 10s. Each person said one number. The first person said 10, the second said 20, and the third said 30.

How many people counted to get to 200? _____
How do you know?

2   Ms. Tan's class counted by 20s. Each person said one number. The first person said 20, the second said 40, and the third said 60.

a. How many people counted to get to 420? _____
How do you know?

b. When Ms. Tan's class counted by 20s, did anyone say the number 300? _____
How do you know?

NOTE

Students work with factors and multiples to solve division problems.
MWI **Multiples: Counting Around the Class**

     © Pearson Education 4

NAME   DATE

Division Practice

Solve the problems. Use equations to show your thinking.
You may also use arrays or pictures of groups.

1   A case of apple juice holds 78 cans. How many 6-packs of apple juice can the case hold?

2   Mr. Yamada's class has 18 students. If the class counts around by a number and ends with 90, what number did they count by?

3 $7\overline{)79}$

4 $112 \div 20$

5   There are 114 students in all of the fourth-grade classes combined. For Field Day, they need to make 9 teams. How many students will be on each team?

NOTE

Students practice solving division problems both with and without story contexts.
MWI **Remainders: What Do You Do With the Extras?**

Multiplication Cluster Problems

Solve the first three or four problems in each cluster. Then solve the final problem, using one or more of the cluster problems (along with other problems if you need them). Show your solution for solving the final problem.

Set A

$4 \times 10 =$

$4 \times 40 =$

$4 \times 3 =$

$2 \times 43 =$

Final problem: **$4 \times 43 =$**

Set B

$5 \times 6 =$

$50 \times 6 =$

$58 \times 2 =$

Final problem: **$58 \times 6 =$**

Set C

$32 \times 2 =$

$10 \times 8 =$

$30 \times 8 =$

Final problem: **$32 \times 8 =$**

Multiplication Cluster Problems

Solve the first three or four problems in each cluster. Then solve the final problem, using one or more of the cluster problems (along with other problems if you need them). Show your solution for solving the final problem.

Set D

$63 \times 10 =$

$60 \times 11 =$

$3 \times 11 =$

Final problem: $\mathbf{63 \times 11} =$

Set E

$5 \times 12 =$

$10 \times 12 =$

$25 \times 6 =$

$50 \times 6 =$

Final problem: $\mathbf{25 \times 12} =$

Set F

$76 \times 10 =$

$70 \times 5 =$

$6 \times 5 =$

Final problem: $\mathbf{76 \times 5} =$

NAME

DATE

Multiplication Pairs

Solve each pair of multiplication problems below. Can you use the first problem to help you solve the second problem?

1 $12 \times 7 =$ _____

$24 \times 7 =$ _____

2 $15 \times 8 =$ _____

$30 \times 4 =$ _____

3 $25 \times 4 =$ _____

$25 \times 8 =$ _____

4 $9 \times 7 =$ _____

$18 \times 7 =$ _____

5 $28 \times 5 =$ _____

$14 \times 10 =$ _____

6 $9 \times 6 =$ _____

$19 \times 6 =$ _____

Ongoing Review

7 Which of the following does not equal 12×8?

Ⓐ 24×4 Ⓑ 2×48 Ⓒ 3×28 Ⓓ 6×16

NOTE

Students practice solving related multiplication problems.
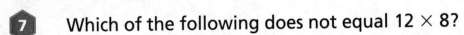 **Multiplication Cluster Problems**

NAME

DATE

Factors and Products 2

Fill in the chart with the missing factors or products. Can you solve some of these mentally?

Factor	×	Factor	=	Product
2	×	54	=	
4	×	27	=	
6	×		=	120
5	×		=	125
3	×	16	=	
7	×		=	84
8	×	60	=	
10	×		=	150
9	×	21	=	

NOTE

Students practice multiplying and dividing.
MWI **Factors and Multiples**

© Pearson Education 4

More Multiplication Problems

Solve these problems. Show your solutions with equations.

1 A yard has 36 inches. How many inches are in 8 yards?

2 A lunar month is 28 days. How many days are in 5 lunar months?

3 A year has 52 weeks. How many weeks are in 4 years?

© Pearson Education **4**

ACTIVITY

More Multiplication Problems

Solve these problems.

4   16 × 4 =

5   24 × 7 =

6   30 × 16 =

7   47 × 3 =

8   23 × 12 =

9   Choose one of the problems above and solve it a
second way, using a different strategy than the one you
used the first time. Explain your strategy with words
or equations.

More Multiplication Problems

Solve these problems.

10   There are 3 teaspoons in a tablespoon. There are 16 times more teaspoons in a cup. How many teaspoons are in a cup?

11   There are 32 fluid ounces in a quart. There are 4 times as many fluid ounces in a gallon. How many fluid ounces are in a gallon?

NAME

DATE

Counting Around the Class 2

1 Ms. Garcia's class counted by 25s. The first person said 25, the second person said 50, and the third said 75. How many people counted to get to 400? _____ How do you know?

2 Mr. Wilson's class counted by 20s. The first person said 20, the second person said 40, and the third said 60. How many people counted to get to 400? _____ How do you know?

3 Ms. Kleinman's class counted by 40s. The first person said 40, the second person said 80, and the third person said 120.

a. How many people counted to get to 400? _____ How do you know?

b. When Ms. Kleinman's class counted by 40s, did anyone say the number 300? _____ How do you know?

NOTE

Students work with factors and multiples to solve division problems.
MWI **Multiples: Counting Around the Class**

NAME

DATE

Solving a Cluster Problem

Solve the three multiplication cluster problems. Then solve the final problem. Explain how you solved the final problem, including which equations from the cluster helped you.

1 Cluster: $7 \times 3 =$

$7 \times 30 =$

$7 \times 4 =$

2 Final problem: $7 \times 34 =$

3 How did you solve 7×34?

NOTE

Students practice solving clusters of familiar multiplication problems, which can help them solve a related problem with larger numbers.

MWI **Multiplication Cluster Problems**

NAME   DATE

Sunken Treasure

Solve the problems. Use another sheet of paper if you need to.
Show equations, pictures, and diagrams you used to solve the
problem. Decide what to do with any extras.

1 There are gold coins found at the site of a shipwreck.
If a scuba diver could carry 18 of these coins to the
surface in one trip, how many trips would it take to
carry 108 coins?

2 If a scuba diver could carry 36 coins to the surface in one
trip, how many trips would it take to carry 108 coins?

3 If five scuba divers found a total of 108 coins and were
allowed to share them equally, how many coins would
each scuba diver get?

4 If the five scuba divers were allowed to share only half
of the 108 coins, how many coins would they each get?

NOTE

Students solve division problems in a real-world context.
MWI Remainders: What Do You Do With the Extras?

Measuring and Classifying Shapes

Measuring and
Classifying Shapes

NAME

DATE

Measurement Benchmarks

Use a ruler, a yardstick, and a meterstick to find objects that are about as long as these measurement units. Record what you find.

Centimeter	Inch	Foot
Example: the tip of my pencil		

Yard	Meter
	Example: the height of the wall from the floor to the board

NAME

DATE

Using Measurement Benchmarks and Measurement Tools

Estimate and measure in inches (to nearest $\frac{1}{4}$ or $\frac{1}{2}$ inch) or centimeters.

Object	Estimate	Actual Measurement
Length of my pencil		
Width of my pencil		
Length of my notebook		

Estimate and measure in feet and inches, or meters and centimeters.

Object	Estimate	Actual Measurement
Height of my desk or table from the floor		
Height of a door in my classroom		
Width of the classroom window		
My teacher's height		

NAME

DATE

Reading Measurement Tools

1 Which is larger, an inch or a centimeter?

2 Which is larger, a meter or a yard?

3 How many millimeters are in one centimeter?

4 How many inches are in one foot?

5 How many centimeters are in one meter?

6 How many feet are in 1 yard?

7 How many millimeters are in 1 meter?

8 How many inches are in 1 yard?

NAME   DATE

Factors and Products

Fill in the chart below with the missing factors or products.
Can you solve these mentally?

	Factor	×	Factor	=	Product
1	6	×	30	=	_____
2	12	×	50	=	_____
3	9	×	_____	=	270
4	5	×	_____	=	300
5	7	×	80	=	_____
6	11	×	_____	=	220
7	8	×	60	=	_____
8	10	×	_____	=	340
9	80	×	4	=	_____

NOTE

Students practice multiplying and dividing multiples of 10.
MWI **Multiplying Groups of 10**

NAME _____ DATE _____

When and How Do You Measure Length?

Ask an adult to tell you about at least four situations in which he or she measures length. Write each situation in one of the boxes. Answer the following questions about each situation.

○ Did you need to measure exactly or estimate?

○ If you estimated, how did you estimate?

○ What tools did you use?

Situation 1:	Situation 2:
Situation 3:	**Situation 4:**

NOTE
_____

Students think about when measurement is used in the real world by adults.

MWI **Linear Measurement**

About Mathematics in This Unit

Dear Family,

Our class is starting a new mathematics unit about geometry and measurement called *Measuring and Classifying Shapes.* During this unit, students measure lengths using U.S. standard units (inches, feet, yards) and metric units (centimeters, meters), convert measurements from larger units to smaller units within the same measurement system (for example, from feet to inches), and measure perimeters. They classify quadrilaterals and triangles based on specific characteristics. They measure angles using other angles as references and using a protractor. Students also solve problems about area, the two-dimensional measure of the size of a surface.

Throughout the unit, students work toward these goals:

Benchmarks	Examples
Benchmark 1: Convert linear measurements from a larger unit to a smaller unit.	Ramona bought 2 yards of fabric. She needs 80 inches of fabric to make a dress. Does she have enough fabric?
Benchmark 2: Determine the perimeter and area of rectangles, including using generalizable methods.	24 in. 8 in. Perimeter = _____ Area = _____
Benchmark 3: Draw and identify lines and angles, including parallel and perpendicular lines, and classify polygons by properties of their sides and angles.	Acute Triangles Right Triangles Obtuse Triangles

About Mathematics in This Unit

Benchmarks	Examples
Benchmark 4: Add or subtract angles to determine the size of angles.	
Benchmark 5: Use a protractor to measure angles and sketch angles of specific sizes.	
Benchmark 6: Identify lines of symmetry in polygons.	

In our math class, students spend time discussing problems in depth and are asked to share their reasoning and solutions. It is important that children solve math problems in ways that make sense to them. At home, encourage your child to explain the math thinking that supports those solutions.

Please look for more information and activities from Unit 4 that will be sent home in the coming weeks.

Converting Classroom Measurements

Use your actual measurements from *Student Activity Book* page 160. Convert your measurement to inches or centimeters. Record your conversion and show your work in the last column.

Object	Measurement in feet and inches, or meters and centimeters	Conversion to inches or centimeters
Height of my desk or table from the floor		
Height of a door in my classroom		
Width of the classroom window		
My teacher's height		

NAME

DATE

Multiplication Problems

Solve each of the problems below. Show your thinking.

1 $22 \times 6 =$ _____

2 $40 \times 14 =$ _____

3 $4 \times 29 =$ _____

4 $36 \times 5 =$ _____

5 $8 \times 26 =$ _____

6 $12 \times 31 =$ _____

NOTE

Students practice solving multiplication problems.

MWI Strategies for Solving Multiplication Problems

NAME   DATE

How Tall Is an Adult?

1 Measure the height of an adult outside of class and then record it. You can record it in feet and inches or in centimeters.

2 Describe what tools you used and how you used the tools to measure the adult.

NOTE

Students practice measuring at home by choosing any measurement tool that they have available.

MWI **Measuring Accurately**

UNIT 4 | **169** | SESSION 1.2   © Pearson Education 4

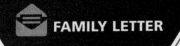
Related Activities to Try at Home

Dear Family,

The activities below are related to the mathematics in the geometry and measurement unit **Measuring and Classifying Shapes**. You can use the activities to enrich your child's mathematical learning experience.

How Long Is It? Look for opportunities for you and your child to estimate and measure lengths and distances in real-life contexts, using both U.S. standard and metric units. You might have your own benchmarks to help you estimate. What do you imagine when you think of a centimeter? A yard? A mile? For instance, you might know that your index fingernail is about a centimeter wide, or that it is a mile to the post office. Show your child how you use various measurement tools in your own measurement activities—hobbies like sewing and carpentry are a natural for this. You and your child can go outside to measure larger distances. How many yards is it to the end of the block? What's the distance in feet between two trees? What would that same distance be in meters?

Building Polygons You and your child can use household materials to create 2-dimensional figures. You can use toothpicks or straws for the sides of your polygons, and small marshmallows, clay, or jelly beans as fasteners for the vertices. How many different kinds of quadrilaterals can you build? How many different kinds of triangles? What different-sized angles can you make?

Related Activities to Try at Home

Symmetry Projects There are many opportunities to notice, name, and discuss symmetry. The world is full of symmetrical objects, both natural and artificial. Look for objects that are symmetrical around the kitchen or outside while on a walk or a drive. You may want to continue exploring symmetrical designs with different art projects.

Your child can print shapes with cut potatoes or sponges dipped in paint on one side of a sheet of paper, and then fold the paper in half. The design that results will be symmetrical around the fold. Paper-cutting is another way to create a symmetrical arrangement of shapes. Plain paper and tissue paper, or newspaper can be folded in quarters (or folded as many times as you like) and then cut and unfolded to create designs with more than one line of symmetry.

NAME   DATE

Perimeters Around the Classroom

Estimate and then find the perimeter of the objects listed below. Choose your own objects for the blank spaces.

Object	Unit of Measure (inches, feet, yards, centimeters, or meters)	Estimate	Actual Measurement
Your classroom door			
Your teacher's desk			
The board			

Converting Lengths Problems

Solve each problem and show how you solved the problem.

1 How many inches are in 4 feet 3 inches? _____

2 Venetta and Bill each made a chain of paper clips and measured their lengths. Venetta's paper clip chain was 3 feet 5 inches long. Bill's chain was 39 inches long. Who had the longer paper clip chain?

3 Derek, Marisol, and Luke together measured the length of the hallway outside their classroom. They each measured a part of the hallway. The part Derek measured was 4 meters long. The part Marisol measured was 32 centimeters long. The part that Luke measured was 5 meters 4 centimeters long. How long is the hallway?

Converting Lengths Problems

4 How many centimeters are in 13 meters 9 centimeters?

_____

5 Noemi and Emaan each measured their teacher's height. Noemi's measurement was 5 feet 7 inches. Emaan's measurement was 67 inches. Did they get the same measurement? Show how you know.

6 Ramona bought 2 yards of fabric. She needs 80 inches of fabric to make a dress. Does she have enough fabric?

7 How many inches are in 2 yards? _____

NAME

DATE

How Long Is Our Classroom?

1 How long is our classroom?

2 What was the most challenging part of measuring our classroom?

© Pearson Education 4

NAME   DATE

What Should We Do with the Extras?

Solve the problems below. Show your work.

1 Noemi is building toy cars. She bought a box of 50 wheels to use on the cars. How many cars can she build with the 50 wheels? How many wheels will she have left?

2 Steve, Jill, Lucy, Ursula, and Terrell earned $106 by raking leaves. They want to share the money equally among the five of them. How much money will each of the friends receive?

3 Juice boxes come in packages of six. The fourth graders at the Glendale School need 82 juice boxes for their field trip to the art museum. How many packages of juice boxes will they have to buy? Explain your answer.

NOTE

Students practice solving division problems and interpreting remainders in a story problem context.

MWI Remainders: What Do You Do With the Extras?

NAME   DATE

Measuring Ribbon

Solve each problem and explain how you did it.

1 Marisol is measuring one piece of ribbon. She will cut it into 17 pieces that are each 9 inches long. How many inches long will the whole piece be?

2 Sabrina is also measuring a piece of ribbon. She needs 22 pieces that are each 13 inches long. How long will her piece of ribbon be?

3 Bill has a piece of ribbon that is 144 inches long. He needs pieces that are 12 inches long. How many pieces can he cut?

NOTE

Students review multiplication and division work in a measurement context.
MWI Division and Multiplication

Perimeters of Rectangles

Solve each problem. Show how you solved the problem.

1

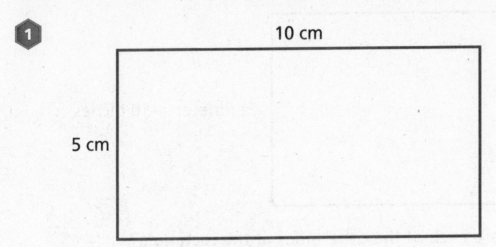

10 cm

5 cm

What is the perimeter of this rectangle?

2 Yuki measured the rectangular top of her desk. The length of the top of her desk is 24 inches. The width of the top of her desk is 18 inches. What is the perimeter of her desk?

3 The field where Marisol plays soccer is a rectangle 100 yards long and 60 yards wide. What is the perimeter of the soccer field?

© Pearson Education 4

Perimeters of Rectangles

4

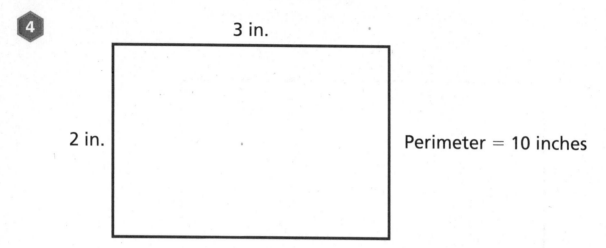

3 in.

2 in.

Perimeter = 10 inches

How long are each of the other sides of the rectangle?

5 Abdul's family wants to plant a garden and put a wood frame around it. They want each side of the garden to be 4 feet long. They have 20 feet of wood. Do they have enough wood to frame the garden? Show how you know.

6 For an art project, Steve had a rectangular piece of paper with a perimeter of 22 inches. Two of the sides were each 6 inches long. How long were each of the other two sides of the paper?

NAME _____ DATE _____

More Perimeters of Rectangles

Solve each problem and show how you solved the problem.

1

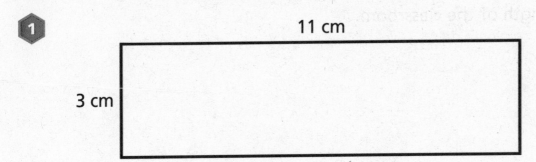

11 cm

3 cm

What is the perimeter of this rectangle?

2 Sabrina bought a rectangular rug that is 15 feet long and 12 feet wide. What is the perimeter of the rug?

3 Ursula's bed is 36 inches wide and 75 inches long. What is the perimeter of Ursula's bed?

NOTE

Students practice solving problems involving the perimeter of rectangles.
MWI **Perimeter or Area?**

NAME

DATE

Explaining Measurement Differences

1 Record all of the measurements your class found for the length of the classroom.

2 What is one of the smallest measurements? _____

3 Why did some people get smaller measurements?

4 What is one of the largest measurements? _____

5 Why did some people get larger measurements?

More Converting Lengths

1 foot	12 inches
1 yard	3 feet
1 meter	100 centimeters

Solve each problem and show how you solved the problem.

1 How many inches in 3 yards? _____

2 Terrell ran around a track that was 100 yards long. How many feet did he run?

3 At the Samson Zoo, there was a python and a boa constrictor. The boa constrictor was 13 feet 8 inches long. The python was 216 inches long. Which snake was longer?

4 How many centimeters in 8 meters?

_____

NOTE

Students solve problems converting measurements from a larger unit to a smaller unit.
MWI Converting Measurement

Polygons, Not Polygons

These are polygons.

 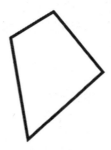 

These are not polygons.

NAME _____   DATE _____

Is It a Polygon?

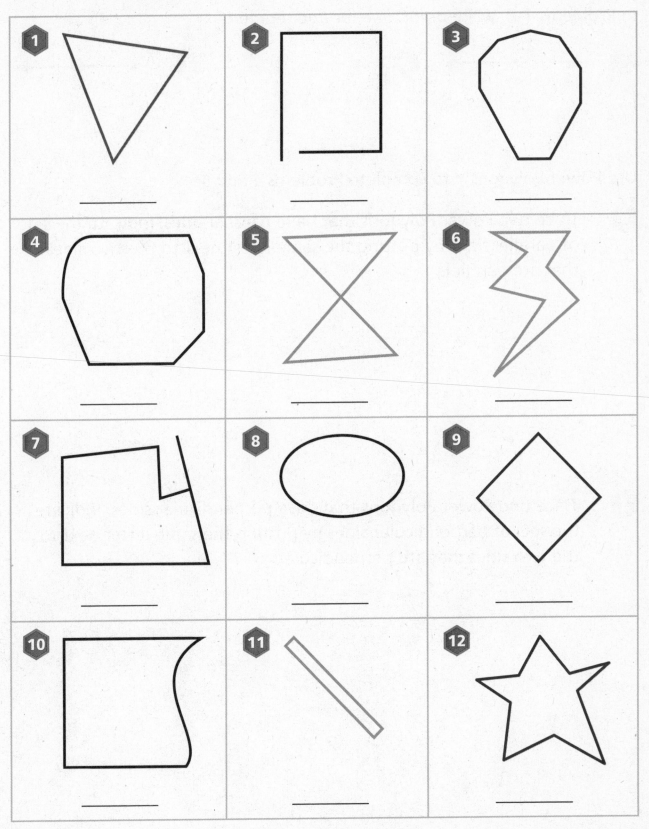

Parallel and Perpendicular Lines

In Problems 1–3, write *point*, *line*, or *line segment*.

Use Power Polygons™ to complete Problems 4 and 5.

4 Trace two Power Polygons that have parallel sides. Indicate the sets of parallel sides by putting the same letter next to the two sides that are parallel.

5 Trace two Power Polygons that have perpendicular sides. Indicate the sets of perpendicular sides by putting the same letter next to the two sides that are perpendicular.

NAME _____ DATE _____

Find the Polygons

Is each shape a polygon? Write **yes** or **no** on the line.

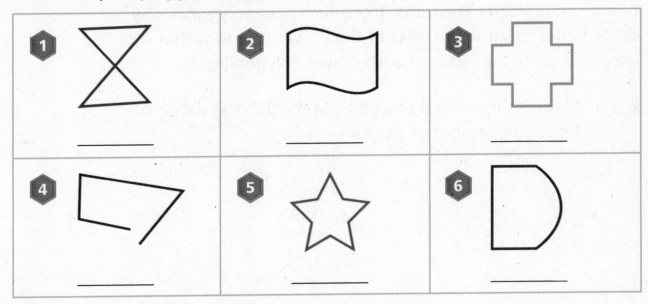

1. _____

2. _____

3. _____

4. _____

5. _____

6. _____

7. Draw two of each shape in the box below.

Polygons	Not Polygons

Ongoing Review

8. Which figure is a triangle?

Ⓐ   Ⓑ   Ⓒ    Ⓓ

NOTE

Students practice identifying polygons as closed shapes with straight sides that do not cross.

MWI **Polygons**

Making Polygons

Follow these directions to make new polygons from two or more Power Polygons. Trace each new polygon. Draw dotted lines to show the sides of the Power Polygons that you used and write the letter of each Power Polygon inside.

1 Make 3 three-sided polygons. Make them as different from one another as you can.

2 Make 3 four-sided polygons. Make them as different from one another as you can.

Making Polygons

Follow these directions to make new polygons from two or more Power Polygons. Trace each new polygon. Draw dotted lines to show the sides of the Power Polygons that you used and write the letter of each Power Polygon inside.

3 Make 2 different five-sided polygons.

4 Make 2 different six-sided polygons.

Making Polygons

Follow these directions to make new polygons from two or more Power Polygons. Trace each new polygon. Draw dotted lines to show the sides of the Power Polygons that you used and write the letter of each Power Polygon inside.

5   Make 2 polygons with at least one set of parallel sides.

6   Make 2 polygons with at least one set of perpendicular sides.

NAME   DATE

Names for Polygons

On the chart, write some words that have prefixes (like "tri" for triangle) that match the prefixes in the names for polygons. You do not have to fill in something for every polygon name.

Number of Sides	Name of Polygon	Words with the Same Prefix
3	Triangle	Example: triathlon (a race with 3 parts)
4	Quadrilateral	
5	Pentagon	
6	Hexagon	
7	Heptagon or Septagon	
8	Octagon	
9	Nonagon	
10	Decagon	
11	Hendecagon	
12	Dodecagon	

NAME   DATE

Division Stories

Write a division equation for each problem. Then, solve each problem and show your work.

1 A case of juice holds 108 cans. How many six-packs of juice does the case hold?

2 Helen has 112 coins in her coin collection. She has 8 times as many coins as Jake has in his collection. How many coins does Jake have in his collection?

3 Mr. Harris's class counted around the class by 20s. The number they ended on was 400. How many students counted?

NOTE

Students practice solving division problems in a story problem context.
MWI Division Situations

NAME _____ DATE _____

Sorting Shapes

Write the numbers of all the shapes that belong in each category.

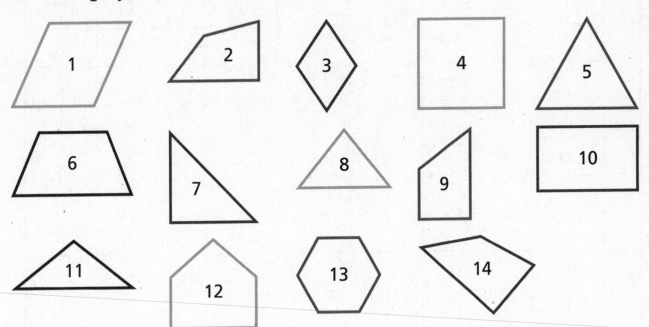

1 Which shapes have at least one pair of parallel sides?

_____

2 Which shapes have at least one pair of perpendicular sides?

_____

3 Which shapes have all sides equal?

_____

NOTE

Students identify parallel sides, perpendicular sides, and sides of equal length in polygons.

MWI Polygons

NAME

DATE

Guess My Rule with Quadrilaterals

Record the rules that you and your partner use as you play *Guess My Rule*. For each rule, write the numbers of the Shape Cards that fit the rule, and the numbers of two or three Shape Cards that do not fit the rule.

Rule	Quadrilaterals That Fit the Rule	Quadrilaterals That Do Not Fit the Rule

Making Quadrilaterals

Make new quadrilaterals that fit each of the descriptions below using two or more Power Polygons. Trace each new polygon. Draw dotted lines to show the sides of the Power Polygons that you used and write the letter of each Power Polygon inside. For each description, try to make at least two different polygons.

1   It is a quadrilateral. It has at least one set of parallel sides.

2   It is a quadrilateral. All of its sides are the same length.

Making Quadrilaterals

Make new quadrilaterals that fit each of the descriptions below using two or more Power Polygons. Trace each new polygon. Draw dotted lines to show the sides of the Power Polygons that you used and write the letter of each Power Polygon inside. For each description, try to make at least two different polygons.

3 It is a quadrilateral. It has at least one set of sides that are perpendicular.

4 It is a quadrilateral. All of its angles are the same size. Not all of its sides are the same length.

ACTIVITY

Making Quadrilaterals

Make new quadrilaterals that fit each of the descriptions below using two or more Power Polygons. Trace each new polygon. Draw dotted lines to show the sides of the Power Polygons that you used and write the letter of each Power Polygon inside. For each description, try to make at least two different polygons.

5 It is a quadrilateral. All of its angles are the same size.

6 It is a quadrilateral. All of its sides are the same length. Not all of its angles are the same size.

NAME   DATE

Mystery Rectangles

1 Draw a line from each Clue Card to the matching rectangle. One of the Clue Cards does not have a matching rectangle.

Clue Card
Clue Card 1 My length is twice as long as my width.
Clue Card 2 My length is 4 units longer than my width.
Clue Card 3 My perimeter is 28 units.
Clue Card 4 All my sides have the same length.
Clue Card 5 The sum of my length and width is a multiple of 10 units.

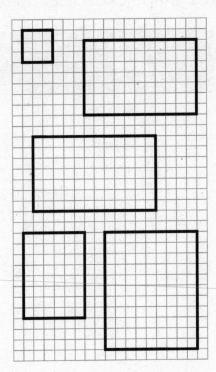

Ongoing Review

2 Which shapes are rectangles?

Ⓐ M and N

Ⓑ T and S

Ⓒ S and O

Ⓓ O and P

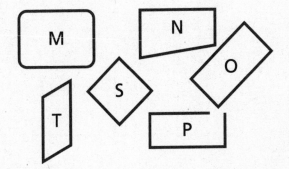

NOTE

Students consider the dimensions of various rectangles.
MWI Quadrilaterals

NAME _____   DATE _____

Guess My Rule with Triangles

Record the rules that you and your partner use as you play *Guess My Rule*. For each rule, write the numbers of the Shape Cards that fit the rule, and the numbers of two or three Shape Cards that do not fit the rule.

Rule	Triangles That Fit the Rule	Triangles That Do Not Fit the Rule

NAME   DATE

Today's Number: Broken Calculator

Find three solutions to each of these problems.

1 I want to make 36 using my calculator, but the 3 key and the 6 key are broken. How can I use my calculator to do this task?

2 I want to make 200 using my calculator, but the 0 key and the + key are broken. How can I use my calculator to do this task?

3 I want to make 64 using my calculator, but the 6 key and the 4 key are broken. How can I use my calculator to do this task?

4 I want to make 55 using my calculator, but the 5 key and the + key are broken. How can I use my calculator to do this task?

NOTE

Students practice building flexibility with all operations (addition, subtraction, multiplication, and division).

MWI **Factors and Multiples**

Sorting Quadrilaterals

Write the numbers of all the quadrilaterals that belong in each category.

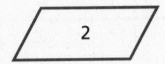
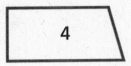
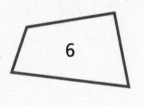

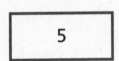
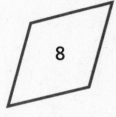

1 Which quadrilaterals have 4 right angles?

_____

_____

2 Which quadrilaterals have 2 pairs of parallel sides?

_____

_____

3 Which quadrilaterals have 4 sides of equal length?

_____

_____

NOTE

Students practice identifying properties in quadrilaterals.
MWI Quadrilaterals

Sorting Quadrilaterals

Draw a shape to prove that each statement below is false.

4   All rectangles are squares.

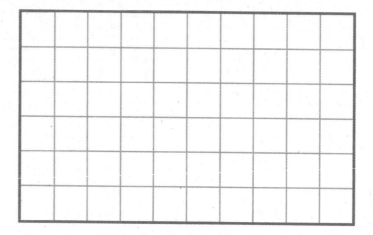

5   All quadrilaterals have at least one right angle.

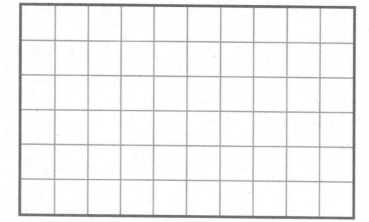

NOTE

Students draw quadrilaterals and correct false statements.
MWI Quadrilaterals

NAME _____ DATE _____

Obtuse, Acute, and Right Angles

Write whether each angle is an obtuse, acute, or right angle.

1

2

3

4

5

6

Sorting Triangles by Angle Size

Write the numbers of the triangle Shape Cards that fit in each category.

Triangles with Only Acute Angles	Triangles with an Obtuse Angle	Triangles with a Right Angle

NAME   DATE

Division and Multiplication Practice

Find the solution to each of these problems.

1 7×24

2 18×4

3 9×30

4 $168 \div 8$

5 $122 \div 7$

6 $269 \div 9$

NOTE

Students practice solving multiplication and division problems.

MWI Division and Multiplication

NAME   DATE

Sides and Angles

For Problems 1 and 2, use the polygon at the right.

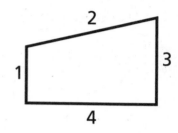

1   Give the numbers for a pair of parallel sides. _____

2   Give the numbers for a pair of perpendicular sides. _____

3   Circle each right triangle.

4   Complete the chart.

	Number of Right Angles	Number of Acute Angles	Number of Obtuse Angles
▭			
▱			
◢			

NOTE

Students identify parallel sides, perpendicular sides, and types of angles in polygons, and they identify right triangles.

MWI Angles and Degrees

Making Right Angles

Use the angles of two or more Power Polygons to make a right angle. Draw the "box" sign to indicate the right angles you create. Trace the polygons that you used and label each with its letter.

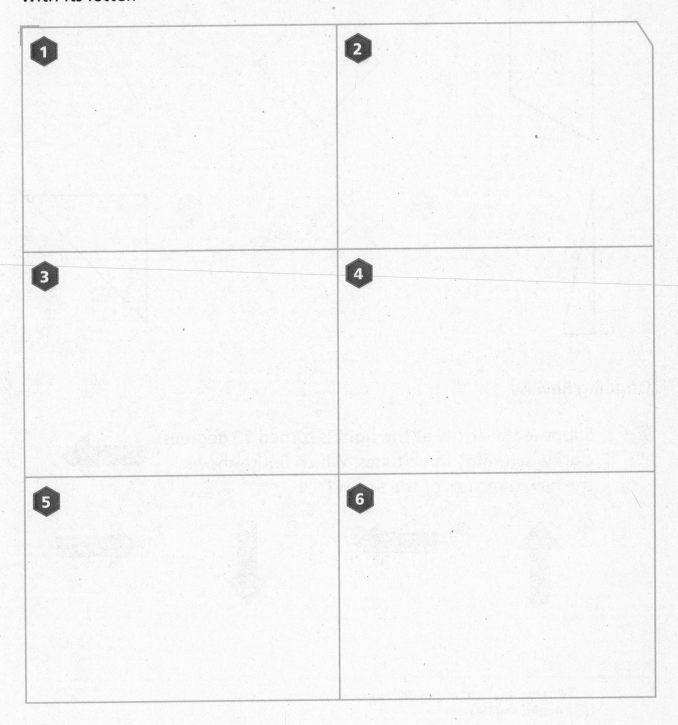

NAME

DATE

Which Angles Are Right Angles?

In each of the polygons below, there is at least one right angle. Find all of the right angles in each polygon and label them with an "R."

 1
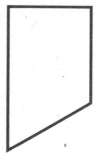

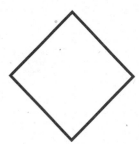 2

3

4

5

6
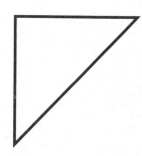

Ongoing Review

7 Suppose the arrow at the right is turned 90 degrees clockwise (right) three times. Which figure shows the new direction of the arrow?

Ⓐ   Ⓑ   Ⓒ   Ⓓ

NOTE

Students identify right angles (90 degree angles).
MWI **Angles and Degrees**

How Many Degrees?

A right angle is measured as 90 degrees. Use the Power Polygons to figure out how many degrees are in each of the angles indicated. Explain your thinking and include any drawings that make your idea clear. If you used addition or subtraction to find the measure of the angle, write an equation.

1 How many degrees is this angle? How do you know?

2 How many degrees is this angle? How do you know?

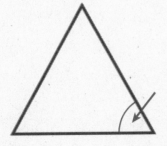

How Many Degrees?

3 How many degrees is this angle? How do you know?

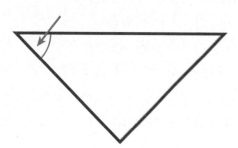

4 How many degrees is this angle? How do you know?

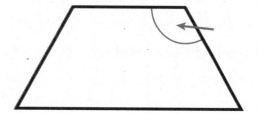

NAME

DATE

Building Angles

Use the angles of two or more Power Polygons to make the angles described. Trace the polygons that you used and label them with their letters. Write an equation that represents how you used the angles in the Power Polygons to make the described angle.

a. Make an angle that measures 60 degrees.

b. Explain how you know that this is a 60° angle.

Equation: _____

c. Can you make another 60° angle with the Power Polygons? Explain how you know.

Equation: _____

Building Angles

Use the angles of two or more Power Polygons to make the angles described. Trace the polygons that you used and label them with their letters. Write an equation that represents how you used the angles in the Power Polygons to make the described angle.

 a. Make an angle that measures 120 degrees.

b. Explain how you know that this is a 120° angle.

Equation: _____

c. Can you make another 120° angle with the Power Polygons? Explain how you know.

Equation: _____

NAME   DATE

Building Angles

Use the angles of two or more Power Polygons to make the angles described. Trace the polygons that you used and label them with their letters. Write an equation that represents how you used the angles in the Power Polygons to make the described angle.

 a. Make an angle that measures 150 degrees.

b. Explain how you know that this is a 150° angle.

Equation: _____

c. Can you make another 150° angle with the Power Polygons? Explain how you know.

Equation: _____

NAME   DATE

Staying Fit

Solve the story problems below. Be sure to show your work and equations.

Marisol's family decided to keep track of how much they exercised during April and May.

1

a. Marisol's mother ran on 22 days in April. On each of those days, she ran 4 miles. How many miles did she run in April?

b. In May, she increased her daily distance to 5 miles, and ran 19 days that month. How many miles did she run in May?

2 At the end of April and May, Marisol calculated that she had walked 3 miles every day for those 61 days. How many miles did she walk in April and May?

3 Marisol's father biked 190 miles in 5 days. He biked the same distance each day. How many miles did he bike each day?

4 Who went more miles in April and May—Marisol's mother or father? How many more miles?

5 How many miles did Marisol's family run, walk, and ride in April and May?

NOTE

Students practice solving multiplication and division problems in a story problem context.
MWI Division and Multiplication

NAME   DATE

Sorting Triangles

Write the numbers of all of the triangles that belong in each category. You may use the corner of a sheet of paper as a "right angle tester."

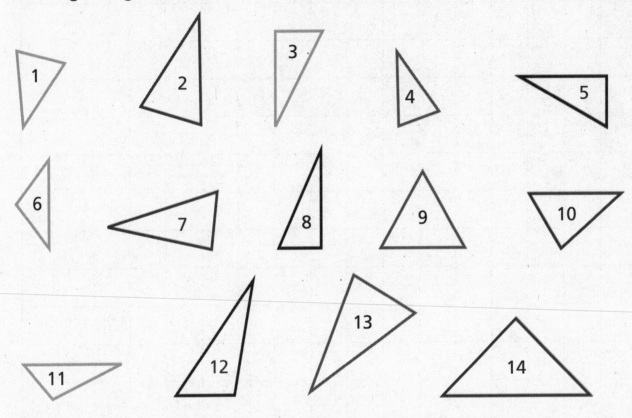

1. Which of the triangles are right triangles?

_____

2. Which triangles have 3 acute angles?

_____

3. Which triangles have 1 obtuse angle?

_____

NOTE

Students practice identifying angles and classifying triangles by their angle sizes.
MWI Classifying Triangles

Measuring with a Protractor

In Problems 1–2, use a protractor to measure each angle.

1

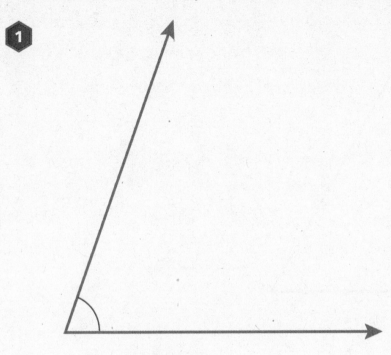

_____ degrees

2

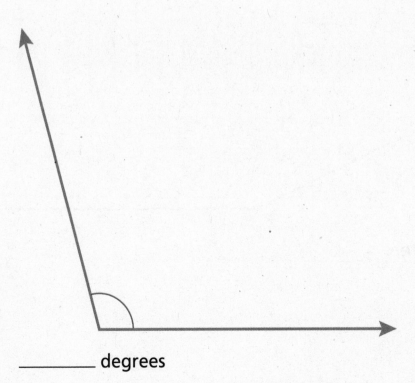

_____ degrees

Measuring with a Protractor

In Problems 3–4, use a protractor to measure each angle.

3

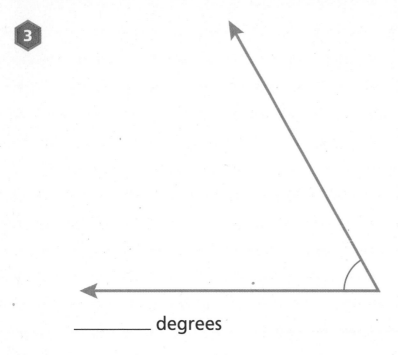

_____ degrees

4

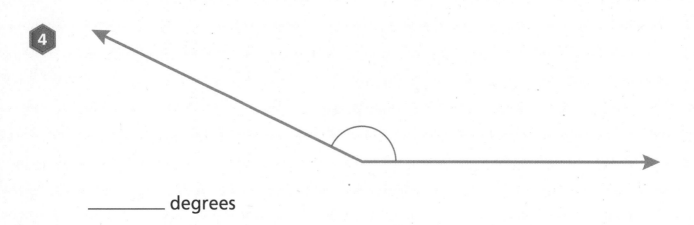

_____ degrees

Measuring with a Protractor

Use a protractor to measure the indicated angle in each polygon.

5

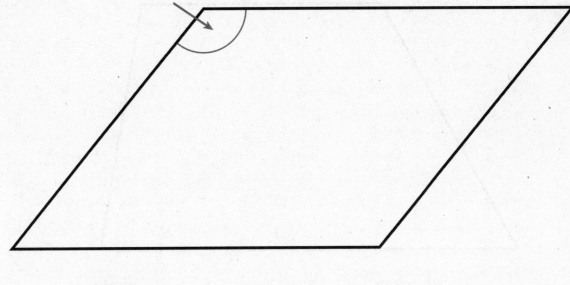

_____ degrees

6

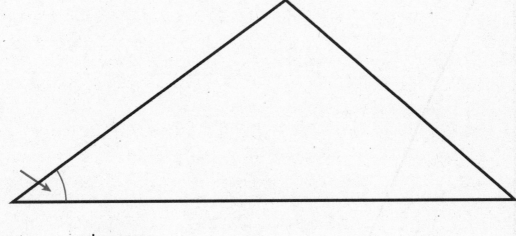

_____ degrees

Measuring with a Protractor

Use a protractor to measure the indicated angle in each polygon.

 7

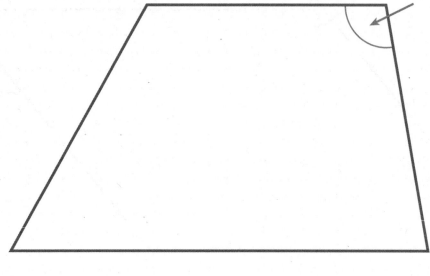

_____ degrees

 8

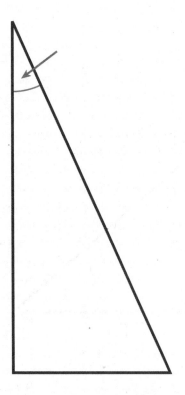

_____ degrees

NAME   DATE   (PAGE 1 OF 2)

Drawing Figures and Measuring Angles

In Problems 1–3, draw an example of the figure.

1 Right triangle

2 Quadrilateral with perpendicular sides

3 Quadrilateral with parallel sides

NOTE

Students draw geometric figures and use a protractor to measure angles.
MWI Measuring with Protractors

Drawing Figures and Measuring Angles

In Problems 4 and 5, use a protractor to measure the indicated angle.

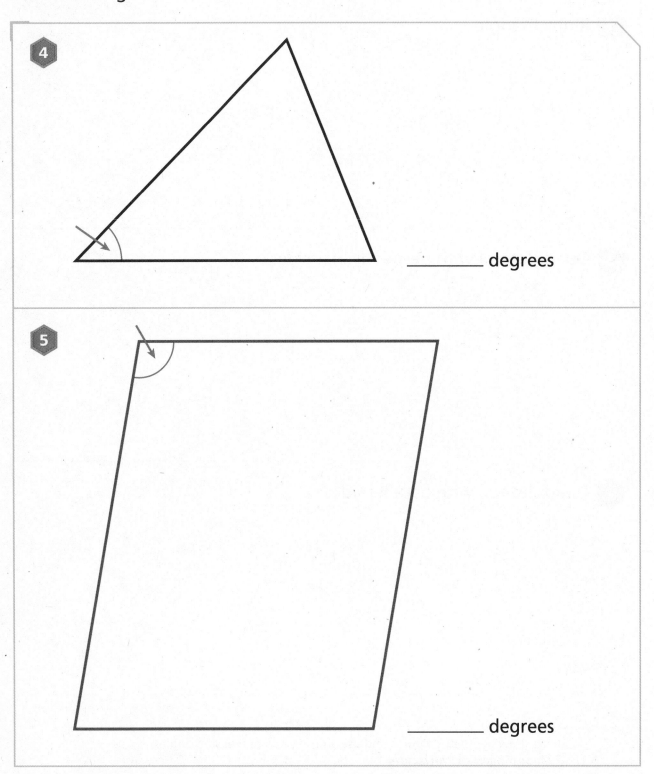

4

_____ degrees

5

_____ degrees

Drawing Lines and Angles

Draw an example of the figure.

1	2	3
Line Segment	**Line**	**Ray**

4	5
Perpendicular Lines	**Parallel Lines**

6	7	8
Right Angle	**Acute Angle**	**Obtuse Angle**

NOTE

Students draw geometric figures.
MWI Points, Line Segments, and Parallel Lines

Drawing Angles and Measuring with a Protractor

For each problem, sketch what you think the given angle looks like. Then use your protractor to draw an angle of the given measurement.

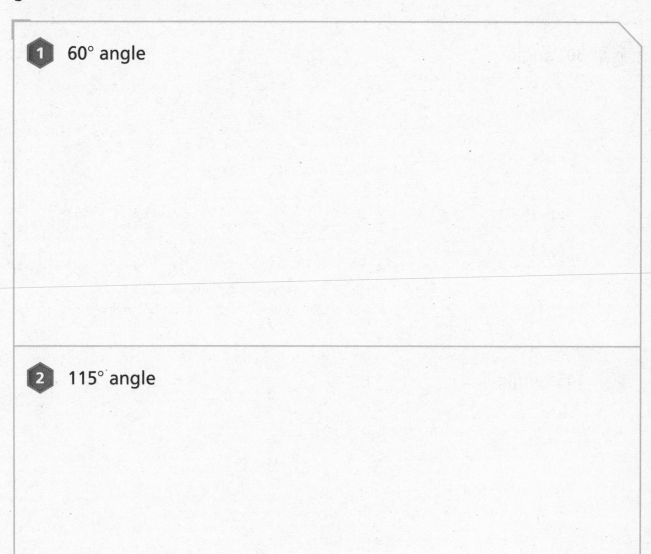

1 60° angle

2 115° angle

Drawing Angles and Measuring with a Protractor

For each problem, sketch what you think the given angle looks like. Then use your protractor to draw an angle of the given measurement.

3 30° angle

4 145° angle

Drawing Angles and Measuring with a Protractor

For each problem, sketch what you think the given angle looks like. Then use your protractor to draw an angle of the given measurement.

5 120° angle

6 75° angle

NAME

DATE

Mystery Multiple Tower

This is the top part of Anna's Multiple Tower. Answer these questions about her tower.

168
154
140
126
112

1 What number did Anna count by?

How do you know?

2 How many numbers are in Anna's tower so far?

How do you know?

3 Write a multiplication equation that represents how many numbers are in Anna's Multiple Tower:

_____ × _____ = _____

NOTE

Students practice solving multiplication and division problems in the context of a "tower" of multiples.

MWI Multiple Towers

Mystery Multiple Tower

4   What is the 10th multiple in Anna's tower?

5   Imagine that Anna adds more multiples to her tower.

     a. What would be the 20th multiple in her tower?

        How do you know?

     b. What would be the 25th multiple in her tower?

        How do you know?

NOTE

Students practice solving multiplication and division problems in the context of a "tower" of multiples.

MWI **Multiple Towers**

NAME

DATE

Measuring Angles

Use the corner of a sheet of paper as a 90-degree angle to help you measure each of the angles below. You may also fold the corner of another sheet of paper in half to make a 45-degree angle with which to measure. Match each angle to one of the measures in the box. One measure is used twice.

| 30° | 45° | 60° | 90° | 120° | 135° | 150° |

1

Angle Measure: _____

2

Angle Measure: _____

3

Angle Measure: _____

4

Angle Measure: _____

5

Angle Measure: _____

6

Angle Measure: _____

7

Angle Measure: _____

8

Angle Measure: _____

NOTE

Students practice identifying angles of particular sizes.

MWI **Measuring with Protractors**

© Pearson Education 4

Directions for Making a Design

Work in pairs to make a symmetrical design.

1 Make a horizontal line of symmetry across the center of Triangle Paper (S44). One side will be the first partner's side; the other will be the second partner's side. Work only on your own side of the line.

2 The first partner places a shape on the triangle paper, touching the line of symmetry on one side.

3 The second partner puts the same kind of shape in the mirror-image position on the other side of the line.

4 The second partner places a new shape on the paper on the second partner's side. The shape must touch either the line of symmetry or at least one corner or side of a shape already placed.

5 The first partner puts a shape in the mirror-image position of the second partner's shape.

6 Continue, until 12 shapes have been placed in all.

7 Set the first design to the side, being sure to keep the pieces in place, and start a new design on a separate sheet of Triangle Paper, following steps 1–6.

8 After you finish the second design, each partner colors one of the designs. Use colors that match the Power Polygon pieces.

Measuring Area with Triangles

Using the triangle piece, determine the area of each of the designs that you made. How many triangles does it take to cover the design?

1   Look at your first design. What is its area? _____

Explain how you determined its area.

2   Look at your second design. What is its area? _____

Explain how you determined its area.

DAILY PRACTICE

Related Problems About Multiplying Groups of 10

Solve each pair of multiplication problems below.

1 9 × 6 = _____

9 × 60 = _____

2 11 × 5 = _____

110 × 5 = _____

3 15 × 6 = _____

15 × 60 = _____

4 14 × 4 = _____

14 × 40 = _____

5 7 × 9 = _____

7 × 90 = _____

6 12 × 6 = _____

12 × 60 = _____

7 5 × 16 = _____

50 × 16 = _____

8 80 × 5 = _____

800 × 5 = _____

NOTE

Students practice solving multiplication problems about multiplying by multiples of 10.

MWI Multiplying Groups of 10

© Pearson Education 4

NAME   DATE

Is It Symmetrical?

Look at each of the block letters below. Some of them have mirror symmetry and some of them do not. For each letter that has mirror symmetry, draw at least one line of symmetry. Can you find more than one line? If a letter does not have a line of symmetry, write "no" next to it.

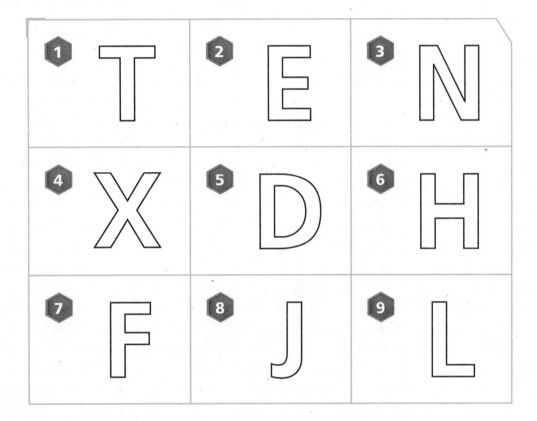

NOTE

Students practice looking for lines of symmetry.
MWI **Mirror Symmetry**

UNIT 4 | **236** | SESSION 4.1   © Pearson Education 4

What's the Area?

Answer the questions.

Build this design with Power Polygons:

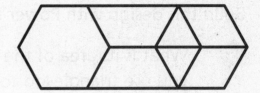

1 What is the area of the design if you use triangles to cover it?

Area: _____ triangles

2 How did you figure out the area?

Build this design with Power Polygons:

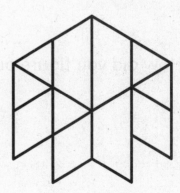

3 What is the area of the design if you use triangles to cover it?

Area: _____ triangles

4 How did you figure out the area?

What's the Area?

Answer the questions.

Build this design with Power Polygons:

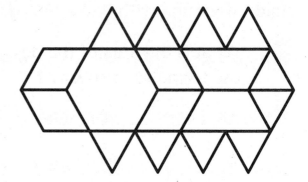

5 What is its area of the design if you use triangles to cover it?

Area: _____ triangles

6 How did you figure out the area?

Mirror Symmetry

For each figure that has mirror symmetry, draw the line(s) of symmetry.

9. On triangle paper, draw a design that has mirror symmetry. You may color it if you like. How many lines of symmetry does your design have?

Ongoing Review

10. In which shape is the dotted line a line of symmetry?

Ⓐ 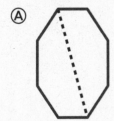 Ⓑ Ⓒ   Ⓓ

Crazy Cakes

Divide each of the Crazy Cakes below into two equal halves. The two halves do not need to have the same shape. Show on the Crazy Cake and explain with words how you know that each person gets $\frac{1}{2}$ of each Crazy Cake.

Crazy Cake 1

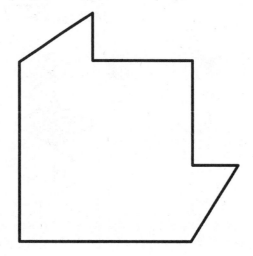

Crazy Cake 2

© Pearson Education **4**

Crazy Cakes

Divide each of the Crazy Cakes below into two equal halves. The two halves do not need to have the same shape. Show on the Crazy Cake and explain with words how you know that each person gets $\frac{1}{2}$ of each Crazy Cake.

Crazy Cake 3

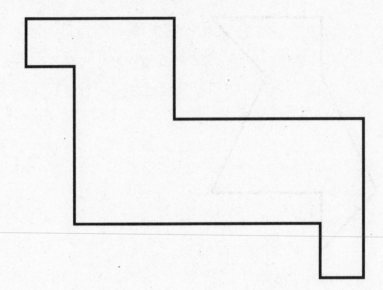

Crazy Cake 4

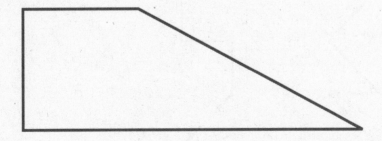

Crazy Cakes

Divide each of the Crazy Cakes below into two equal halves. The two halves do not need to have the same shape. Show on the Crazy Cake and explain with words how you know that each person gets $\frac{1}{2}$ of each Crazy Cake.

Crazy Cake 5

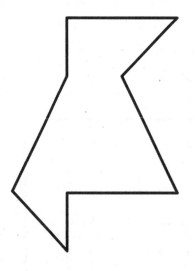

Crazy Cake 6

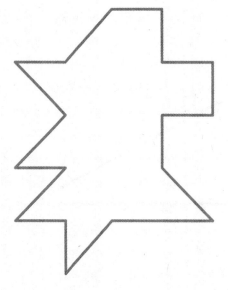

NAME _____ DATE _____

More Lines and Angles

In Problems 1–3, draw an example of the figure.

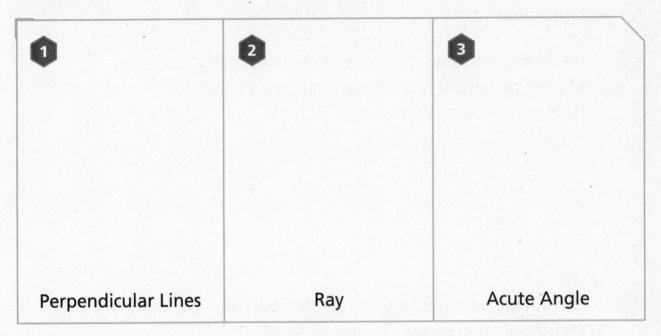

①	②	③
Perpendicular Lines	Ray	Acute Angle

④ Use a protractor to measure each numbered angle.

Angle 1 _____ degrees

Angle 2 _____ degrees

Angle 3 _____ degrees

Angle 4 _____ degrees

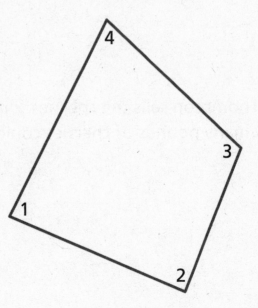

NOTE

Students draw geometric figures and use a protractor to measure angles.

MWI Points, Line Segments, and Parallel Lines

More Multiplication and Division Stories

Solve each problem and show your work. Write an equation for each problem.

1 Ms. Thompson sold 6 cartons of cherries at the Farmers' Market on Saturday. Each carton holds 25 cherries. How many cherries did she sell?

2 On Sunday, Ms. Thompson sold 300 cherries. How many cartons of cherries did she sell on Sunday?

3 Ms. Thompson sells the cherries for $4 per pound. How many pounds of cherries could you buy for $50?

NOTE

Students practice solving multiplication and division problems in a story problem context.
MWI Division and Multiplication

Area of Polygons

Each square is 1 square centimeter. Determine the area of each polygon in square centimeters. Explain or show how you found the area.

1

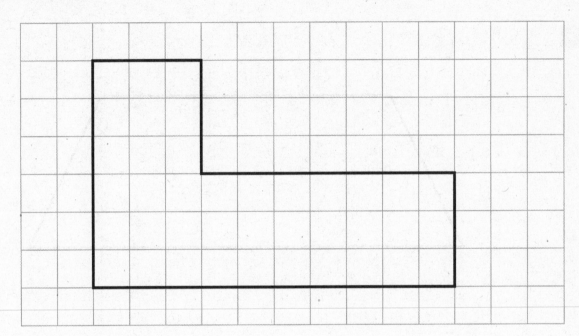

2

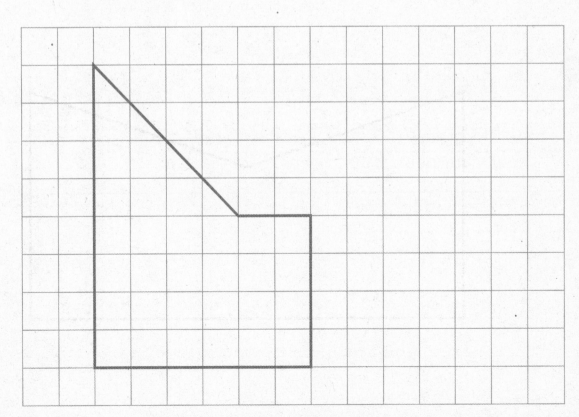

Area of Polygons

Each square is 1 square centimeter. Determine the area of each polygon in square centimeters. Explain or show how you found the area.

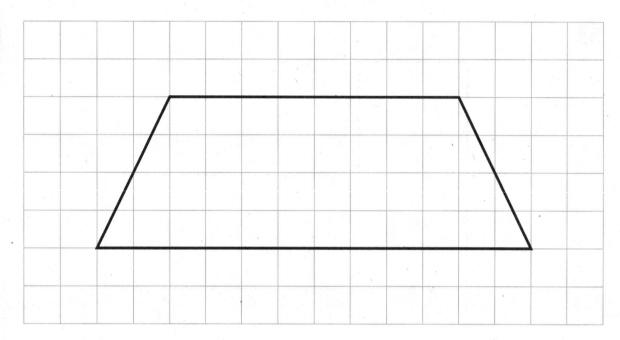

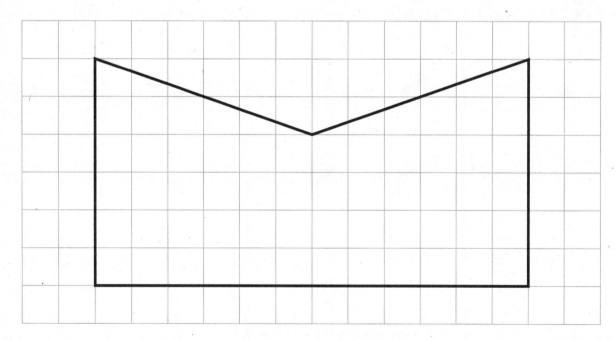

Area of Polygons

Each square is 1 square centimeter. Determine the area of each polygon in square centimeters. Explain or show how you found the area.

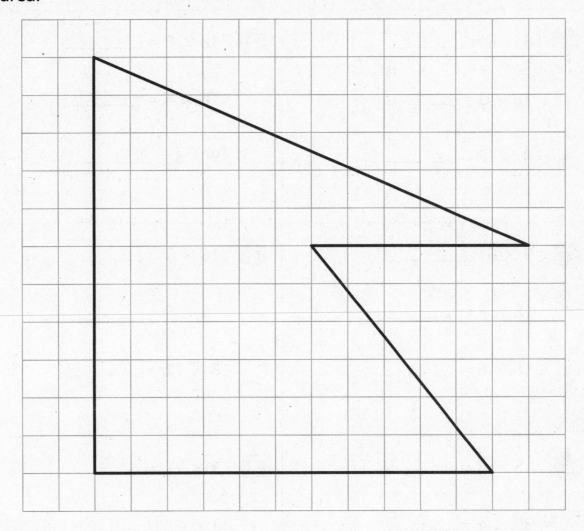

NAME

DATE

Related Problems About Doubling and Halving

Solve each set of multiplication problems below.

1 8 × 6 = _____

16 × 3 = _____

4 × 12 = _____

2 18 × 8 = _____

18 × 4 = _____

9 × 8 = _____

3 9 × 6 = _____

18 × 3 = _____

18 × 6 = _____

4 16 × 3 = _____

16 × 6 = _____

8 × 12 = _____

5 15 × 8 = _____

30 × 4 = _____

60 × 4 = _____

6 3 × 21 = _____

3 × 42 = _____

6 × 42 = _____

NOTE

Students practice solving multiplication problems. Ask your child to explain any patterns he or she notices in each set of problems.

MWI **Multiplication Cluster Problems**

NAME

DATE

That's Not Fair!

1 Draw an "X" on any shape that is not fairly divided into two equal halves.

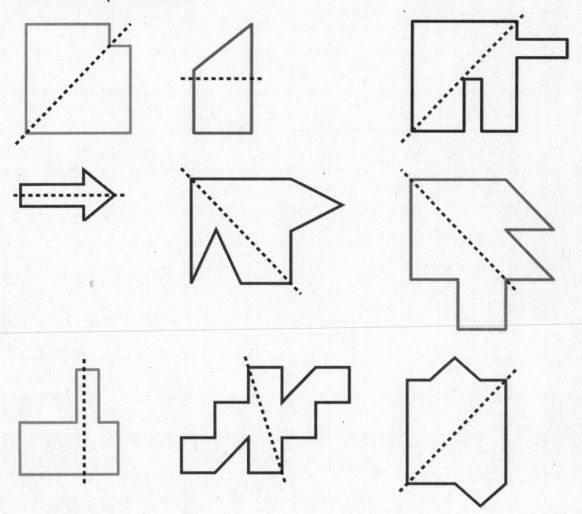

2 Choose one of the shapes above that does not have equal halves and explain how you know.

NOTE

Students decide whether the two parts of irregular shapes have equal areas.
MWI Mirror Symmetry

Partially Covered Rectangles

The part of Mr. Frank's classroom that is tiled is covered with rugs. In the drawings below, each tile is one square foot. Find the area of each section of tiled floor. Explain how you got your answer.

 1   Area: _____

Explain.

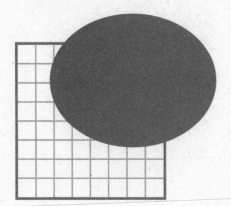

2   Area: _____

Explain.

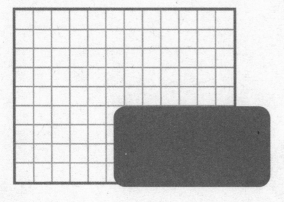

Partially Covered Rectangles

The part of Mr. Frank's classroom that is tiled is covered with rugs. In the drawings below, each tile is one square foot. Find the area of each section of tiled floor. Explain how you got your answer.

3 Area: _____

Explain.

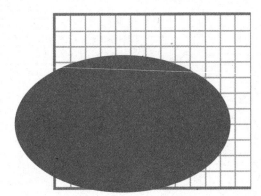

4 Area: _____

Explain.

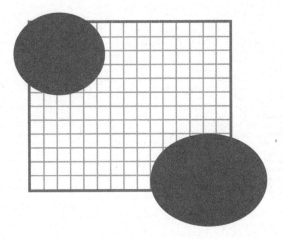

Area of Rectangles

Determine the area or the missing dimension of each rectangle.
Show how you figured out the area or the missing dimension.

1

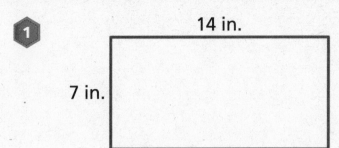

14 in.

7 in.

What is the area of the rectangle?

2 Jill and Benson have a rectangular vegetable garden
that is 23 feet by 5 feet. Venetta has a rectangular garden
that is 18 by 8 feet. Which garden has a larger area?
How many square feet larger is it?

3

16 cm

6 cm

What is the area of the rectangle?

Area of Rectangles

4

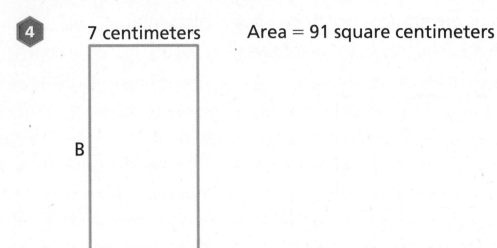

7 centimeters   Area = 91 square centimeters

B

What is the length of side B?

5 Amelia has a rectangular rug in her room that is 12 feet long. The area of the rug is 96 square feet. What is the width of the rug?

6 The basketball court at the Rockway School is a rectangle 84 feet by 50 feet. What is the area of the basketball court?

More Measuring Angles with a Protractor

Use a protractor to measure the angles.

1

2

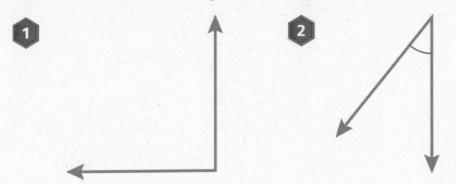

3

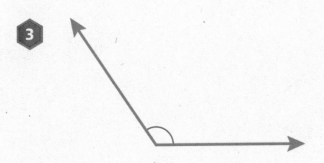

NOTE

Students practice using a protractor to measure angles.

MWI **Measuring with Protractors**

More Measuring Angles with a Protractor

Use a protractor to measure the indicated angles.

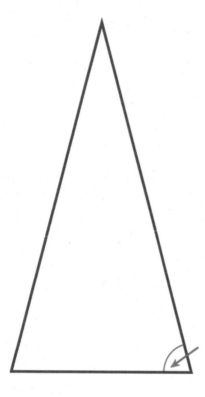

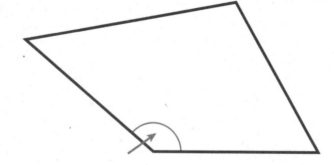

NAME _____   DATE _____

More Area of Rectangles

Determine the area or the missing dimension of each rectangle.
Show how you figured out the area or the missing dimension.

1

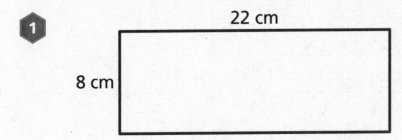

22 cm

8 cm

What is the area of the rectangle?

2 The Greatest Comics Store hosts game nights in a
rectangular room that is 14 feet by 18 feet. Future Games
has a rectangular room for playing and testing games
that is 17 feet by 15 feet. Which room has a larger area?
How many square feet larger is it?

3 Perfect Pizza has a small rectangular parking lot that is
25 feet long and 12 feet wide. What is the area of the
parking lot?

4 Archie's model railroad is on a large table that is
14 feet long. The area of the table is 84 square feet.
What is the width of the table?

NOTE

Students find the area of rectangles, or are given one dimension and the area of
a rectangle, and asked to find the missing dimension.
MWI Finding Area of a Rectangle

Large Numbers and Landmarks

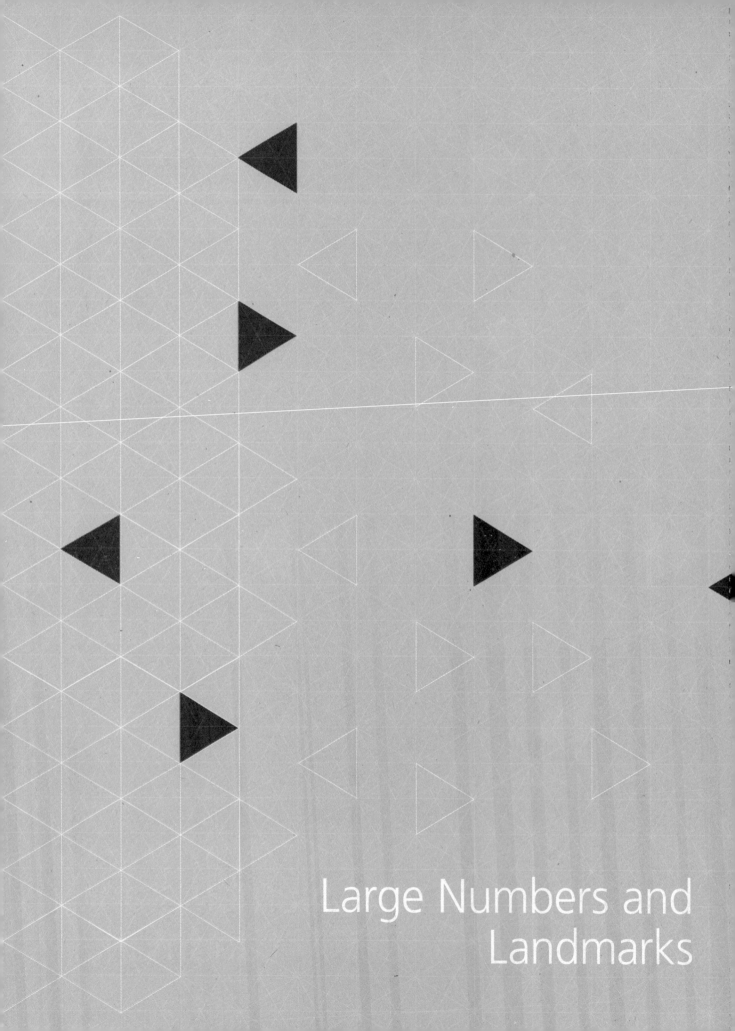

Large Numbers and
Landmarks

The Jones Family's Trip

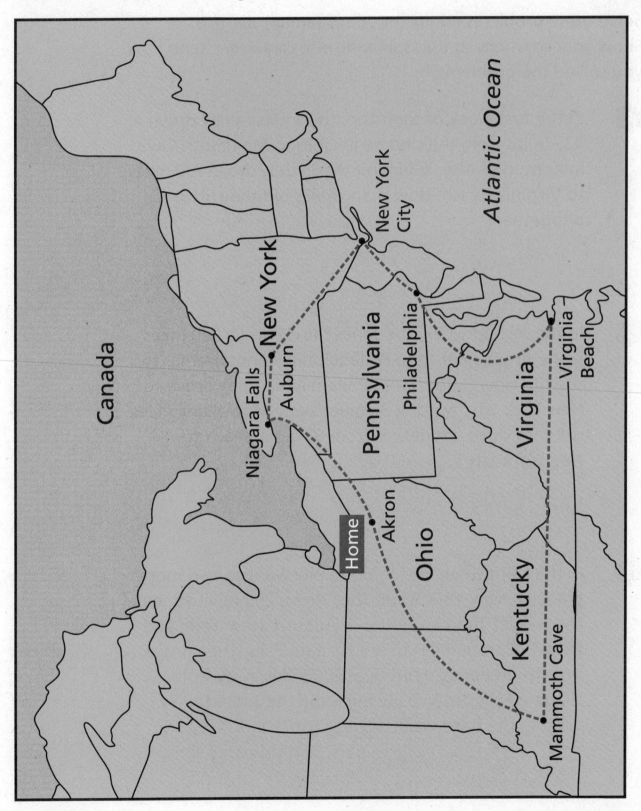

Atlantic Ocean

New York City

New York

Philadelphia

Pennsylvania

Virginia

Virginia Beach

Auburn

Niagara Falls

Canada

Home

Akron

Ohio

Kentucky

Mammoth Cave

How Many Miles?

Solve these problems about the Jones family's car trip.
Show your solutions so that someone else can understand how
you solved the problems.

1   In the first week of their trip, the Jones family drove
427 miles from their home in Ohio to Mammoth Cave
in Kentucky. After their visit there, they drove 733 miles
to Virginia Beach. How many miles did they drive
altogether?

2   In the second week, the Jones family drove 270 miles
from Virginia Beach to Philadelphia, Pennsylvania, to
see the Liberty Bell. From Philadelphia, they drove to
New York City, which is 96 miles away. How many miles
did they drive altogether from Virginia Beach to
New York City?

3   In the third week, the Jones family went to two more
places in New York state. They drove 259 miles to see
the Harriet Tubman House in Auburn, New York, and
then 138 more miles to see Niagara Falls. Then it was
time to go home, which was 235 miles away from
Niagara Falls. How many miles did the Jones family
drive in the third week of their trip?

NAME

DATE

Count Your Change Carefully

Complete this chart.

Item	Cost of Item	Amount Given to Clerk	Amount of Change
1 Ruler	$0.47	$1.00	
2 Sandwich	$3.18	$5.00	
3 Seeds	$1.55		$0.45
4 Socks	$2.74		$2.26
5 Shampoo		$1.00	$0.11
6 Apple		$5.00	$4.10
7 Stickers	$1.16	$10.00	
8 Magazine		$10.00	$6.35

Ongoing Review

9 $255 + \underline{\hspace{1.5cm}} = 1{,}000$

Ⓐ 755　　Ⓑ 750　　Ⓒ 745　　Ⓓ 705

NOTE

Students practice addition and subtraction in the context of money and receiving change.
MWI Subtraction Problem Types

NAME

DATE

Addition Problems

Solve the following addition problems and show your solutions. (Try to use a new strategy that you learned in class today.)

1 At the Harriet Tubman House in Auburn, New York, the Jones family spent $9.45 for all their admission tickets and $6.99 for a book about Tubman's life. How much money did they spend at the Harriet Tubman House?

2 $488 + 522 = $ _____

3
```
  534
+ 327
-----
```

NOTE

Students practice strategies for solving addition problems.
MWI Addition Strategies

NAME   DATE

About the Mathematics in This Unit

Dear Family,

Our class is starting a new addition and subtraction unit, *Large Numbers and Landmarks*. During this unit, students study place value in large numbers, and complete a final study of addition and subtraction strategies. Students are expected to leave Grade 4 using a variety of strategies, including the U.S. standard algorithms, to fluently solve multidigit addition and subtraction problems.

Throughout the unit, students work toward these goals:

Benchmark/Goal	Examples
Read, write, and compare numbers up to 1,000,000 and round them to any place.	68,094 Expanded form: $60,000 + 8,000 + 90 + 4$ Words: sixty-eight thousand, ninety-four Rounded to nearest 10,000: 70,000 Rounded to nearest 1,000: 68,000 Rounded to nearest 100: 68,100 Rounded to nearest 10: 68,090
Fluently solve multidigit addition and subtraction problems using a variety of strategies including the U.S. standard algorithms.	$451 - 287 =$ **Solution 1** 13 151 287 300 451 **Solution 2** $\begin{array}{r} \overset{3}{\cancel{4}}\ \overset{14}{\cancel{5}}\ \overset{11}{\cancel{1}} \\ -\ 2\ 8\ 7 \\ \hline 1\ 6\ 4 \end{array}$

NAME

DATE

About the Mathematics in This Unit

Benchmark/Goal	Examples
Use addition and subtraction to solve word problems involving measurement.	*Carmen flies from Los Angeles to Mexico City, which is 4,771 kilometers. From Mexico City she flies to Rio de Janeiro, which is 7,678 kilometers. How far does she fly altogether?*

In our math class, students spend time discussing problems in depth and are asked to share their reasoning and solutions. It is important that children solve math problems accurately and efficiently in ways that make sense to them. At home, encourage your child to explain the math thinking that supports those solutions.

Please look for more information and activities about *Large Numbers and Landmarks* that will be sent home in the coming weeks.

NAME   DATE

More Addition Problems

Solve the following addition problems and show your solutions.
(Try to use a strategy that you have not tried before.)

1 The Jones family stopped at a pizza place for supper.
They ordered a large pizza that cost $12.95. They also
shared a salad that cost $7.49. How much did supper
cost that night?

2 While they were driving, Mrs. Jones gave Donte this
problem to solve: 458 + 548. His answer was 1,006.
Did he get the right answer? Show how you would
solve this problem.

3 457 + 776 = _____

More Addition Problems

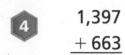 4   1,397
    + 663

 5   353
    + 918

6    $582 + 434 = $ _____

NAME   DATE

Solving Addition Problems

Solve each addition problem. Show your work clearly.

1 639 + 541 = _____

2 739 + 541 = _____

3
```
  186
+ 805
```

Ongoing Review

4 Which number does **not** have a 7 in the ones place?

Ⓐ 7   Ⓑ 17   Ⓒ 470   Ⓓ 977

NOTE

Students practice solving addition problems.
MWI Addition Strategies

NAME _____ DATE _____

Even More Addition Problems

Solve the following addition problems and show your solutions.

1 Tara saved $143 from babysitting and opened a bank account. During the year, she put $829 more in the account. How much money did she have in the bank at the end of the year?

2 Marcos went to the store to buy materials for his science fair project. The poster board cost $7.99 and the packet of construction paper cost $2.49. How much money did he spend?

3 536 + 887 = _____

NOTE

Students continue to solve addition problems.
MWI **Addition Strategies**

UNIT 5 | **270** | SESSION 1.2   © Pearson Education 4

Addition Starter Problems

For each problem below, three different ways to start are shown. Solve each start. Then choose one of the starts and use it to solve the rest of the problem.

1   Problem: 315 + 566 = _____

315 + 500 = _____

300 + 500 = _____

300 + 566 = _____

2   Problem: 288 + 456 = _____

288 + 400 = _____

200 + 400 = _____

300 + 456 = _____

3   Problem: 597 + 375 = _____

597 + 300 = _____

500 + 300 = _____

600 + 372 = _____

Addition Starter Problems

4 Problem: $9.94 + $5.16 = _____

$9.94 + $5.00 = _____

$9.00 + $5.00 = _____

$0.94 + $0.06 = _____

5 Problem: 785 + 428 = _____

785 + 400 = _____

700 + 400 = _____

800 + 428 = _____

NAME

DATE

Related Problems about Multiplying Groups of 10

Solve each pair of multiplication problems below.

1 $8 \times 6 =$ _____

$8 \times 60 =$ _____

2 $7 \times 7 =$ _____

$7 \times 70 =$ _____

3 $9 \times 7 =$ _____

$90 \times 7 =$ _____

4 $12 \times 8 =$ _____

$120 \times 8 =$ _____

5 $15 \times 5 =$ _____

$15 \times 50 =$ _____

6 $6 \times 13 =$ _____

$60 \times 13 =$ _____

7 $11 \times 4 =$ _____

$11 \times 40 =$ _____

8 $60 \times 5 =$ _____

$600 \times 5 =$ _____

Ongoing Review

9 Which is 400 less than 866?

Ⓐ 862   Ⓑ 826   Ⓒ 466   Ⓓ 422

NOTE

Students practice solving multiplication problems about multiplying groups of 10.

 **Multiplying Groups of 10**

NAME

DATE

How Do You Solve an Addition Problem?

To the student:

1 Solve this problem and show your solution:

299 + 156 = _____

To the adult:

2 How would you solve this problem? Please record your solution. (If you solved the problem mentally, explain what you did.)

$$\begin{array}{r} 299 \\ + \ 156 \\ \hline \end{array}$$

3 Is the way you solved Problem 2 the way you were taught to solve addition problems when you were in school? __YES __NO

If not, show the way you were taught here:

$$\begin{array}{r} 299 \\ + \ 156 \\ \hline \end{array}$$

NOTE

Students practice solving addition problems. Share with your child how you would solve the problem.

MWI Addition Strategies

Related Activities to Try at Home

Dear Family,

The activities below are related to the mathematics in this addition and subtraction unit, *Large Numbers and Landmarks*. You can use the activities to enrich your child's mathematical learning experience.

Making Sense of Large Numbers

With your child, look for large numbers in the newspaper, on packages, on signs, and around your home and neighborhood. Talk together and ask questions about the numbers. You might ask, "How much would the car cost if the salesperson offered a $2,500 discount?"

You might ask, "If 45,000 people went to the basketball game at Central Stadium last night, how many seats were empty?"

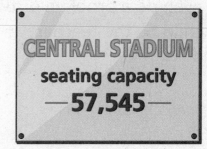

CENTRAL STADIUM
seating capacity
—57,545—

Related Activities to Try at Home

Adding and Subtracting Distances

Find opportunities to give your child first-hand experiences with distances, such as the number of miles driven across town or on a long trip. If you drive, show your child the odometer on your car, and ask your child to help you figure out how far it is to the grocery store or the playing field. You might ask, "If we start at 24,538 miles, and when we get to the store the odometer reads 24,542, how far have we gone?"

How Did You Solve That?

Ask your child to tell you about how he or she is adding and subtracting. Show that you are interested in these approaches. Because these strategies may be unfamiliar to you, listen carefully to your child's explanation; you might even do a problem or two, using the new procedure. Let your child be the teacher!

Two Different Solutions

1 Solve this problem. Show your solution, using clear and concise notation.

$$145 + 229 = \underline{\hspace{2cm}}$$

Now look carefully at these two different solutions for the same problem. Answer the questions below.

Solution 1

$$
\begin{array}{r}
145 \\
+\,229 \\
\hline
300 \\
60 \\
+\,14 \\
\hline
374
\end{array}
$$

Solution 2

$$
\begin{array}{r}
\overset{1}{1}45 \\
+\,229 \\
\hline
374
\end{array}
$$

2 How would you explain to someone else how Solution 1 works? Where does the 300 come from? Where does the 60 come from? Where does the 14 come from?

3 How would you explain to someone else how Solution 2 works? Where does the 1 above the 4 in 145 come from?

NAME   DATE

Applying the U.S. Standard Algorithm for Addition

Choose two of these numbers. Add them using the U.S. standard algorithm and check your answer using a different method. If you have time, try another pair of numbers.

489	683	354	218	807	1,394

NAME

DATE

Solving an Addition Problem in Two Ways

1 Solve this problem in two different ways. Be sure to show how you got your answer.

431 + 799 = _____

Here is the first way I solved it:

Here is the second way I solved it:

Ongoing Review

2 Which of the following is true?

Ⓐ 11 + 880 > 1,000   Ⓑ 642 + 419 > 1,000

Ⓒ 733 + 218 > 1,000   Ⓓ 82 + 904 > 1,000

NOTE

Students practice strategies for addition by solving a problem in two ways.
MWI **Addition Strategies**

Practicing the U.S. Standard Algorithm for Addition

Use the U.S. standard algorithm to solve each problem.
Check your answers by using another method.

1
```
  462
+ 384
```

2
```
  548
+ 327
```

3 $687 + 215 =$

Practicing the U.S. Standard Algorithm for Addition

4 Yuki collected 241 stamps. Luke collected 289 stamps. How many stamps have they collected all together?

5
```
  1,044
+   572
```

6
```
  2,373
+   488
```

NAME

DATE

Apple Orchard

Solve the story problems below. Show your work and
your equations.

1 At an apple orchard, small bags contain 7 apples.
Alexa and her family bought 91 apples for a party.
How many small bags did they buy?

2 Large bags hold 14 apples. When a fourth-grade class
went apple picking, they filled 9 large bags. How many
apples did they pick?

3 Savanna and her three brothers picked 55 apples.
They shared the apples equally among the four of them.
How many apples did each child get? Were there any
apples left over?

NOTE

Students practice solving multiplication and division problems in story problem contexts.
MWI **Division and Multiplication**

© Pearson Education 4

NAME   DATE

Adding to 1,000

Fill in the missing number in each equation. Show how you found the missing number.

1 $1{,}000 = 635 +$ _____

2
$$
\begin{array}{r}
289 \\
+ \underline{} \\
1{,}000
\end{array}
$$

3   _____ $+ 543 = 1{,}000$

NOTE

Students create addition problems that add to 1,000.
MWI **Place Value: Large Numbers**

NAME _____ DATE _____

Related Problems about Doubling and Halving

Solve each set of multiplication problems below.

1   4 × 7 = _____

8 × 7 = _____

8 × 14 = _____

2   6 × 9 = _____

12 × 9 = _____

6 × 18 = _____

3   3 × 11 = _____

6 × 11 = _____

6 × 22 = _____

4   5 × 8 = _____

10 × 8 = _____

20 × 8 = _____

5   3 × 15 = _____

3 × 30 = _____

6 × 15 = _____

6   32 × 4 = _____

16 × 8 = _____

8 × 8 = _____

NOTE

Students practice solving multiplication problems.
MWI Multiplication Cluster Problems

© Pearson Education 4

Subtraction Word Problems

Draw a picture or number line to show what is happening in each story. Then solve each problem and show your solution.

1 Jamie's family visited their grandmother, who lives 634 miles from their house. On the first day, they drove 319 miles. How many miles did they have left to drive the second day?

2 Mr. Rivera and Ms. Santos each drove from Boston to other cities. Mr. Rivera drove 446 miles to Washington, D.C. Ms. Santos drove 1,300 miles to Orlando. How many more miles did Ms. Santos drive?

3 Ms. Jones took a trip from Washington, D.C., to Dallas, Texas, which is 1,329 miles away. She stopped in Nashville, which is 666 miles from Washington, D.C., and then drove to Dallas. How many miles did she drive from Nashville to Dallas?

Subtraction Word Problems

4 Andreas had 475 basketball cards in his collection. He gave 189 cards to his younger brother for his birthday. How many cards does Andreas have left?

5 Natasha had $8.72. She spent $4.89 on a gift for her mother. How much money does Natasha have left?

6 Riverside School has 557 girls and 463 boys. How many more girls than boys are at the school?

NAME   DATE

Subtraction Problems

Solve each subtraction problem. Show your work clearly.

1 $1,200 - 635 =$ _____

2 $884 - 591 =$ _____

3
$$
\begin{array}{r}
771 \\
-\ 258 \\
\hline
\end{array}
$$

Ongoing Review

4   Which of the following is true?

    Ⓐ $618 - 117 < 500$ Ⓑ $733 - 234 > 500$

    Ⓒ $956 - 455 > 500$ Ⓓ $876 - 375 < 500$

NOTE

Students practice solving subtraction problems.
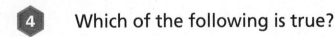 Subtraction Strategies

NAME _____ DATE _____

Close to 1,300

Read the story below and answer the questions.

Robert and Leslie are playing a game they made up called Close to 1,300. The object of the game, as in *Close to 1,000*, is to think of two numbers with a total that is as close to 1,300 as possible.

1 Robert thought of this combination:

937 + 365

What is Robert's total? _____

2 Leslie thought of this combination:

424 + 856

What is Leslie's total? _____

3 Who is closer to 1,300? _____

4 What is each person's score? (Remember that the score is the difference between the total and 1,300.)

Robert's score: _____   Leslie's score: _____

NOTE

Students solve addition problems to create a sum close to 1,300.
MWI **Place Value: Large Numbers**

© Pearson Education **4**

Solving Subtraction Problems

Solve each problem and show your solution.

1 631 − 268 = _____

2
$$\begin{array}{r} 704 \\ -\ 551 \\ \hline \end{array}$$

3 Jenna has 826 stamps in her collection. Ricardo has 637 stamps in his collection. How many more stamps does Jenna have than Ricardo?

ACTIVITY

Solving Subtraction Problems

4 The Diamond Egg Farm had 1,321 chickens. Last month they sold 663 of them to another farm. How many chickens do they have left?

5 In 1985, the population of West Littlebury was 1,877 people. In 2005, the population was 2,391 people. By how many people did the population of West Littlebury increase from 1985 to 2005?

6 $4,495 - 2,504 =$ _____

NAME   DATE

What's the Story?

Write a story to go with each problem. Then solve the problem and show your solution.

1
$$947$$
$$-\ 182$$

2 $1{,}253 - 940 =$ _____

3 $714 - 399 =$ _____

NAME _____ DATE _____

What Should We Do with the Extras?

Solve the problems below and show your solutions.

1 Joey and his aunt picked 72 apples at the orchard. They plan to put them in bags of 5 apples each. How many bags of apples can they fill?

2 Five friends earned a total of $72 from washing cars. They want to share the money equally among the 5 of them. How much money will each of the friends receive?

3 Glue sticks come in packages of 5. The art teacher at the Glendale School needs 72 glue sticks in her classroom. How many packages of glue sticks will she need to buy?

NOTE

Students practice solving division problems and interpreting remainders in story problem contexts.

MWI Remainders: What Do You Do With the Extras?

© Pearson Education 4

NAME

DATE

Addition Practice

Solve the problems below and show your solutions. Use the U.S. standard algorithm for addition for at least one of the problems.

1
$$\begin{array}{r} 272 \\ + 354 \\ \hline \end{array}$$

2 768 + 843 = _____

3 Cesar took his mom out to lunch. They shared a pizza, which cost $9.78, and they shared a salad, which cost $4.29. Cesar's mom had coffee, which cost $1.10. How much did Cesar spend for lunch?

NOTE

Students continue to practice adding 3-digit numbers.
MWI U.S. Standard Algorithm for Addition

© Pearson Education 4

NAME

DATE

Events at the Community Center

Many events are held at the community center. Here are some events and the attendance at these events.

Event	Attendance
Science Fair	368
Basketball Tournament	741
Book Fair	555
Swim Meet	496
Rock Concert	1,152
Homecoming Dance	783

1 What was the total attendance at the science fair and the rock concert?

2 Which event had more people in attendance, the homecoming dance or the swim meet? How many more?

3 a. Which 3 events had the highest attendance?

b. What was the total attendance at those 3 events?

NOTE

Students solve addition and subtraction problems in a story context.
MWI Multi-Step Problems With Larger Numbers

The U.S. Standard Algorithm for Subtraction

Use the U.S. standard algorithm for subtraction to solve the following problems. Then solve the problems using a different strategy to double-check your answers.

1
```
   757
 − 428
```

2
```
   361
 − 143
```

The U.S. Standard Algorithm for Subtraction

3 There are 893 students at the Mills School. Some students bring their lunch from home, and the others eat the school lunch. On Tuesday, 158 students brought their lunch from home. How many students had the school lunch?

4
```
   678
 − 386
```

NAME   DATE

Using the U.S. Standard Algorithm

Use the U.S. standard algorithm for subtraction to solve each problem. Use another strategy to double-check your answers.

  1

$$
\begin{array}{r}
498 \\
-\ 279 \\
\hline
\end{array}
$$

  2

$$
\begin{array}{r}
525 \\
-\ 164 \\
\hline
\end{array}
$$

NOTE

Students practice strategies for subtraction by solving problems in two ways, including the U.S. standard algorithm.

MWI U.S. Standard Algorithm for Subtraction

Subtraction Starter Problems

For each problem below, four different ways to start are shown. Choose two of the starts and use each one to solve the rest of the problem.

1 397 − 139 =

397 − 100 =   139 + 61 =   397 − 140 =

$$\begin{array}{r} {}^{8\ 17} \\ 3\cancel{9}\cancel{7} \\ -\ 1\ 3\ 9 \\ \hline \end{array}$$

First way: Second way:

2
$$\begin{array}{r} 847 \\ -\ 652 \\ \hline \end{array}$$

847 − 600 =   652 + 48 =   847 − 700 =

$$\begin{array}{r} 847 \\ -\ 652 \\ \hline 5 \end{array}$$

First way: Second way:

Subtraction Starter Problems

3   1,458 − 297 =

$$1{,}458 - 200 = \qquad 297 + 3 = \qquad 1{,}458 - 300 = \qquad \begin{array}{r} 1458 \\ -\ 297 \\ \hline 1 \end{array}$$

First way: Second way:

4 $$\begin{array}{r} 3{,}363 \\ -\ 1{,}418 \\ \hline \end{array}$$

$$3{,}363 - 1{,}000 = \qquad 1{,}418 + 1{,}000 = \qquad 1{,}418 + 82 = \qquad \begin{array}{r} ^{5\ 13} \\ 33\cancel{6}\cancel{3} \\ -\ 1418 \\ \hline \end{array}$$

First way: Second way:

NAME

DATE

Solving Subtraction Problems

Use the U.S. standard algorithm for subtraction to solve each problem. Check each of your answers by using another method.

 487 − 209 = _____

Here is how I solved it using the U.S. standard algorithm:

Here is the second way I solved it:

 1,265 − 795 = _____

Here is how I solved it using the U.S. standard algorithm:

Here is the second way I solved it:

NOTE

Students practice strategies for subtraction by solving a problem in two ways, including the U.S. standard algorithm.

MWI Subtraction Strategies

NAME   DATE

Solving More Addition Problems

Use the U.S. standard algorithm for addition to solve each problem. Check each of your answers by using another method.

  $667 + 358 =$ _____

Here is how I solved it using the U.S. standard algorithm:

Here is the second way I solved it:

  $1,304 + 2,889 =$ _____

Here is how I solved it using the U.S. standard algorithm:

Here is the second way I solved it:

NOTE

Students practice strategies for addition by solving a problem in two ways, including the U.S. standard algorithm.

MWI U.S. Standard Algorithm for Addition

ACTIVITY

Distances from Chicago

Employees at the Pascal Moving Company move people from Chicago, Illinois, to other parts of the United States. Use the mileage chart below to answer the following questions. Show all your work. Remember that all trips begin in Chicago.

City	Distance (in miles) from Chicago, IL	City	Distance (in miles) from Chicago, IL
Albuquerque, NM	1,335	Phoenix, AZ	1,800
Boston, MA	1,015	Salt Lake City, UT	1,403
Las Vegas, NV	1,761	San Francisco, CA	2,148
Miami, FL	1,377	Seattle, WA	2,072
New Orleans, LA	929	Washington, D.C.	715

1 Avery is driving the truck to Phoenix. He has driven 552 miles. How many miles is he from Phoenix?

Distances from Chicago

2   Olivia is driving to San Francisco. If she is 1,674 miles from San Francisco, how far has she driven?

3   Avery is driving to Salt Lake City. On the first day, he drove 325 miles, and on the second day, he drove 459 miles. How far is he from Salt Lake City?

4   One week, Olivia drove to Boston. For her next trip, she drove to Seattle. How many more miles did she drive for the second trip?

5   Olivia drives to Las Vegas and Avery drives to Albuquerque. How many more miles does Olivia drive than Avery?

   © Pearson Education **4**

Practicing the U.S. Standard Algorithm for Subtraction

Use the U.S. standard algorithm to solve each problem. Then solve the same problem using a different strategy and compare your answers.

1
$$\begin{array}{r} 587 \\ -\ 260 \\ \hline \end{array}$$

2 $738 - 465 =$

3 Mr. Valdez drove 901 miles to see his niece. Ms. Jones drove 342 miles to see her mother. How much farther did Mr. Valdez drive?

Practicing the U.S. Standard Algorithm for Subtraction

4 Juan had 589 marbles in his collection. A friend gave him some more marbles, and now he has 1,964 marbles. How many marbles did his friend give him?

5
```
   5,706
 − 3,438
```

More Subtraction Starter Problems

For each problem below, four different ways to start are shown. Choose two of the starts and use each one to solve the rest of the problem.

1 $805 - 694 =$

$$805 - 600 = \qquad 694 + 6 = \qquad 805 - 700 = \qquad \begin{array}{r} 805 \\ -694 \\ \hline 1 \end{array}$$

First way: Second way:

2 $1{,}363 - 779 =$

$$1{,}363 - 700 = \qquad 1{,}363 - 363 = \qquad 779 + 21 = \qquad \begin{array}{r} \overset{5\,13}{13\cancel{6}\cancel{3}} \\ -779 \\ \hline \end{array}$$

First way: Second way:

NOTE

Students solve subtraction problems using different starts.
MWI Subtraction Strategies

NAME

DATE

Mystery Tower

The picture shows the top part of Richard's multiple tower. Answer these questions about his tower.

192
176
160
144
128

1 What number did Richard count by? How do you know?

2 How many numbers are in Richard's tower so far? How do you know?

3 Write a multiplication equation that represents how many numbers are in Richard's multiple tower.

_____ × _____ = _____

NOTE

Students practice solving multiplication and division problems.
MWI Multiple Towers

© Pearson Education 4

Mystery Tower

4 What is the 10th multiple in Richard's tower?

5 Imagine that Richard adds more multiples to his tower.

a. What would be the 20th multiple in his tower?
How do you know?

b. What would be the 25th multiple in his tower?
How do you know?

Ongoing Review

6 $8,350 - 400 + 60 =$ _____

Ⓐ 8,110   Ⓑ 8,100   Ⓒ 8,010   Ⓓ 8,001

NAME   DATE

Addition and Subtraction Practice

Solve the problems below and show your solutions.

1 The U.S. Olympic Soccer Team played in several cities around the United States. They played their first game in Los Angeles and then flew to Denver, which is 1,018 miles away. After the Denver game, they flew to Dallas, which is 879 miles from Denver. How many miles did the team travel?

2 A new player joined the team. She flew straight from Los Angeles to Dallas, which is 1,434 miles away. How many fewer miles did she travel than the team?

NOTE

Students practice solving addition and subtraction problems.
MWI Subtraction Strategies

NAME   DATE

Division Stories

Solve each problem below. Show your work.
Write a division equation for each problem.

1 A theater ticket costs $8. How many tickets can you buy for $128?

2 Each row in a theater has 12 seats. If 132 students go to see a play at the theater, how many rows of seats can they fill?

3 If 132 students ride to the theater in vans, and 6 students can ride in each van, how many vans will they need?

Ongoing Review

4 Which expression is **less than** 500?

Ⓐ 490 + 80 − 30 − 10 − 10   Ⓒ 595 − 200 + 300

Ⓑ 868 − 400 + 20   Ⓓ 420 + 300 − 100 − 90

NOTE

Students practice solving division problems in story problem contexts.
MWI Division Strategies

Shark Attack!

Shown below are sharks found around the world and their typical weights, in pounds.

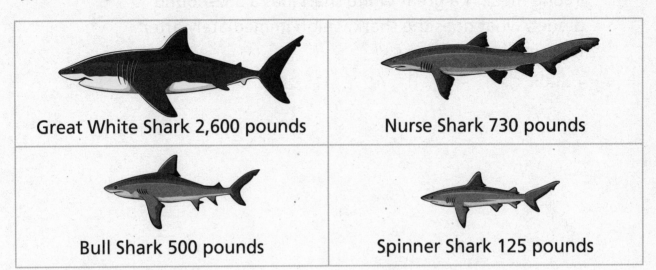

Great White Shark 2,600 pounds	Nurse Shark 730 pounds
Bull Shark 500 pounds	Spinner Shark 125 pounds

Answer the following questions, using the information shown above. Try to do some of the problems mentally. Show your written work on another sheet of paper.

1 A Florida fisherman caught a bull shark and a spinner shark. What is the combined weight?

2 Some newspapers reported that a great white shark with a weight of 7,032 pounds was caught off the coast of Cuba in 1945. Some scientists, however, think that the story is just a fish tale. What is the difference between the weight of the legendary Cuban great white shark and the weight of a typical great white shark?

NOTE

Students practice solving addition and subtraction problems.
MWI **Place Value: Large Numbers**

Shark Attack!

3 A great white shark can eat as much as 400 pounds in one meal. If a great white shark has a 352-pound dinner, what does the shark weigh immediately after finishing its meal?

4 Three 180-pound men are fishing for sharks. Which of these is a heavier load: 3 men, a nurse shark, and 2 spinner sharks; or 3 men, 2 bull sharks, and a spinner shark? How did you get your answer?

NAME   DATE

How Many 10s Are in 10,000?

From your work on the 10,000 chart, you know that:

There are ten 1,000s in 10,000.
There are one hundred 100s in 10,000.

How would you explain to a Grade 3 student how many tens there are in 10,000?

Write your explanation on a separate sheet of paper. You may write it as a letter to a Grade 3 student if you wish. You may also include any pictures or equations that you think will help make your explanation clearer.

NAME

DATE

Writing and Rounding Numbers

For Problems 1–3, write the number in expanded form. Then round it to the given place.

1 8,402
Expanded form:
Round to nearest 100:
Round to nearest 1,000:

2 3,595
Expanded form:
Round to nearest 100:
Round to nearest 1,000:

3 6,840
Expanded form:
Round to nearest 100:
Round to nearest 1,000:

For Problems 4 and 5, write the number in words. Then round it to the given place.

4 9,091
Number name:
Round to nearest 100:
Round to nearest 1,000:

5 10,501
Number name:
Round to nearest 100:
Round to nearest 1,000:

NOTE

Students use place-value understanding to write numbers in expanded form and to round numbers.

MWI Rounding Large Numbers

ACTIVITY

NAME _____   DATE _____

Stadium and Arena Capacities

The following table shows the seating capacities of a number of fictitious stadiums and arenas. Use the data in the table to complete pages 320–322 and pages 325–328.

Stadiums and Arenas		
Grand Canyon Stadium	Tempe, AZ	73,521
Garden State Stadium	East Rutherford, NJ	78,741
Gopherdome	Minneapolis, MN	64,035 (football) 55,883 (baseball) 40,000 (concerts)
Empire Stadium	New York, NY	57,545
Sunshine Stadium	Los Angeles, CA	56,000
Cajundome	New Orleans, LA	69,703 (football) 20,000 (concerts) 55,675 (basketball) 63,525 (baseball)
Patriot Park	Boston, MA	33,993
Copper State Arena	Phoenix, AZ	19,023
Jersey Arena	East Rutherford, NJ	20,049
Big Apple Arena	New York, NY	19,763
Minutemen Center	Boston, MA	18,624 (basketball) 19,600 (concerts)
Badger Arena	Milwaukee, WI	18,600 (basketball) 20,000 (concerts)
Golden State Arena	Los Angeles, CA	20,000

UNIT 5 | **319** | SESSION 3.3

© Pearson Education 4

Filling Up and Emptying

Use the data about stadium and arena capacities on page 319 to solve Problems 1–10 on pages 320–322. Remember to show the equations you use to solve the problems. You should be able to do most of these problems mentally.

In Problems 1–3, people are going to a sold-out basketball game at the Golden State Arena.

1   The game starts at 7:30 P.M. At 7:00 P.M., 9,000 people are in their seats. How many people are not yet in their seats?

2   **a.** At 7:45 P.M., 5,000 more people have arrived and are in their seats. How many people are now in their seats?

       b. How many people are not yet in their seats?

3   At 8:00 P.M., all but 1,500 people are in their seats. How many people are now in their seats?

Filling Up and Emptying

In Problems 4–6, people are going to a football game at the Gopherdome.

4 The game is sold out. At the end of the third quarter, the game is not close, so 10,000 people go home. How many people are still in the stadium?

5 With 10 minutes left in the game, 20,000 more people go home. How many people are still in the stadium?

6 At the end of the game, another 25,000 people leave. The others stay to wait for the traffic to clear. How many people are still in the stadium?

Filling Up and Emptying

In Problems 7–10, people are going to a football game at the Cajundome.

7 Of the available tickets, there were 2,500 tickets that were not sold. How many tickets were sold?

8 At 6:00 P.M., 10,000 people were in the Cajundome. How many people were not yet in the stadium? (Remember, not all seats were sold.)

9 a. At 7:00 P.M., 37,800 more people had come into the stadium. How many people were in the stadium at that time?

b. How many people had not shown up yet? (Remember, not all seats were sold.)

10 Eventually, everyone who had a ticket had come to the game. At halftime, 25,000 people were not in their seats. How many people were still seated?

NAME _____ DATE _____

Rounding Large Numbers

In Problems 1 and 2, round each number to the nearest thousand.

1 2,716 _____   **2** 8,325 _____

In Problems 3 and 4, round each number to the nearest ten thousand.

3 781,407 _____   **4** 97,300 _____

In Problems 5 and 6, round each number to the nearest hundred thousand.

5 570,003 _____   **6** 116,325 _____

7 Round each population to the nearest ten thousand.

City	Population	Nearest Ten Thousand
Austin, TX	786,382	
Cleveland, OH	431,363	
Oakland, CA	409,184	

8 Suppose a number is rounded to the nearest hundred thousand.

What is a number less than 700,000 that rounds to 700,000? _____

What is a number greater than 700,000 that rounds to 700,000? _____

NOTE

Students use place-value understanding to round numbers up to 1,000,000.
MWI **Rounding Large Numbers**

NAME _____ DATE _____

Concert Tickets

Use the data about the number of concert tickets sold.

Holiday Rock Concert	413,125 tickets
Summer Jazz Concert	418,832 tickets

1 Write the number of tickets sold in expanded form.

Holiday Rock Concert: _____

_____

Summer Jazz Concert: _____

_____

2 Round the number of tickets sold to the nearest ten thousand.

Holiday Rock Concert: _____

Summer Jazz Concert: _____

3 Round the number of tickets sold to the nearest hundred thousand.

Holiday Rock Concert: _____

Summer Jazz Concert: _____

4 Compare the number of tickets sold. Use $<$, $>$, or $=$.

413,125 _____ 418,832

NOTE

Students use place-value understanding to write numbers in expanded form, round numbers, and compare numbers through 1,000,000.
MWI **Place Value: Large Numbers**

Rock On!

Use the data about stadium and arena capacities on page 319 to solve Problems 1–13 on pages 325–328. Record how you solved the problems, using clear and concise notation.

The Composites, the hottest rock band in the United States, have decided to go on tour. Their good friends, the Square Roots, will be the opening band.

1 The Composites are deciding whether they should play Jersey Arena or Big Apple Arena. How many more seats are there in Jersey Arena than in Big Apple Arena?

2 The band decides to play both Jersey Arena and Big Apple Arena. They sell all the tickets for both concerts. How many tickets are sold?

3 How many more tickets would the band sell if they sold out at Garden State Stadium instead of at Grand Canyon Stadium?

4 The Composites and the Square Roots play sold-out concerts at the Gopherdome, Sunshine Stadium, and the Minutemen Center. How many tickets did they sell for these three concerts?

ACTIVITY

Rock On!

In Problems 5–8, the Composites and the Square Roots decide to play a benefit concert at Empire Stadium that starts at 3:00 P.M.

5 At 2:00 P.M., 40,895 people are already in the stadium. How many more people can the stadium hold?

6 a. At 3:00 P.M., as the Square Roots start to play, 12,472 more people have arrived. How many people are in the stadium now?

b. How many more people can the stadium hold?

7 By 4:00 P.M., every seat has been taken. As the Composites are setting up, 49,083 people are in their seats, and the others have gone to the concession stands. How many people are at the concession stands?

8 38,012 people buy souvenirs at the concert. How many people do not buy souvenirs?

Rock On!

9 The Composites and Square Roots play sold-out concerts at Patriot Park and Copper State Arena. How many tickets were sold for these two concerts?

10 The bands sell all but 500 tickets for an 8:00 P.M. concert at Badger Arena. At 7:30 P.M., 18,777 people have arrived. How many people are not yet at the arena?

11
a. The bands play a sold-out concert at Minutemen Center. At 7:00 P.M., 11,456 people are in the arena. At 7:30 P.M., 6,845 more people have arrived. How many people have not shown up?

b. Everyone has finally arrived at the concert at Minutemen Center. After the Square Roots play, 4,219 people leave their seats to buy refreshments or souvenirs. How many people are still in their seats?

Rock On!

In Problems 12 and 13, the Composites and the Square Roots play a sold-out concert at Grand Canyon Stadium that begins at 5:00 P.M.

12
a. At 4:00 P.M., 62,106 people are in the stadium. How many more people are expected to show up?

b. At 4:30 P.M., 10,500 more people have arrived. How many people are at the concert now?

c. How many people have not yet arrived?

13 As the Composites start to play, everyone has arrived. 64,086 people are in their seats, and the others are at the concession stands. How many people are at the concession stands?

Traveling the World

Carmen is traveling the world. Use the U.S. standard algorithm for addition to solve the following problems.

1 Carmen flies from Los Angeles to Mexico City (4,771 kilometers) and from Mexico City to Rio de Janeiro (7,678 kilometers). How far does she fly altogether?

2 Carmen flies from New York City to Paris (5,807 kilometers) and from Paris to Cape Town (9,345 kilometers). How far does she fly altogether?

3 Carmen flies from Montreal to Lisbon (6,915 kilometers) and from Lisbon to Tokyo (11,130 kilometers). How far does she fly altogether?

4 Carmen flies from San Francisco to Honolulu (3,851 kilometers) and from Honolulu to Hong Kong (8,930 kilometers). How far does she fly altogether?

Use the answers above to compare the distances of the trips.
Use <, >, or = in the middle blank to show the comparison.

5 Trip 1 total: _____ _____ Trip 2 total: _____

6 Trip 3 total: _____ _____ Trip 4 total: _____

Traveling the World

Diego has to make numerous business trips from his home in Chicago. Use the table below and the U.S. standard algorithm for subtraction to solve the following problems.

Distance from Chicago to Other Cities (in miles)							
Buenos Aires	5,598	Hong Kong	7,784	Honolulu	4,248	London	3,950
Paris	4,134	Rome	4,808	Shanghai	7,081	Sydney	9,272

7 One week Diego flies from Chicago to Paris. The next week he flies from Chicago to Buenos Aires. How much farther is it from Chicago to Buenos Aires than from Chicago to Paris?

8 On his next trip, Diego flies from Chicago to Shanghai. After that he flies from Chicago to Rome. How much farther is it from Chicago to Shanghai than from Chicago to Rome?

9 Next, Diego flies from Chicago to Honolulu. Two weeks later he flies from Chicago to London. How much farther is it from Chicago to Honolulu than from Chicago to London?

10 For his final business trips, Diego first flies from Chicago to Sydney. The next month, he flies from Chicago to Hong Kong. How much farther is it from Chicago to Sydney than from Chicago to Honk Kong?

NAME _____ DATE _____

Areas of Countries

In Problems 1–4, use the data about the areas of some countries.

Austria	32,382 square miles
Indonesia	741,096 square miles
Chile	292,258 square miles

1 Write each country's area in expanded form.

Austria: _____

Indonesia: _____

Chile: _____

2 Round Austria's area to the nearest ten thousand. _____

3 Round Indonesia's area to the nearest thousand. _____

4 Round Chile's area to the nearest hundred thousand. _____

5 Write three numbers that would round to 520,000 when rounded to the nearest ten thousand.

_____

NOTE

Students use place-value understanding to write numbers in expanded form and round numbers through 1,000,000.
MWI Rounding Large Numbers

NAME _____ DATE _____

Practicing Addition and Subtraction

Solve the following problems using the U.S. standard algorithms for addition and subtraction.

1   34,500 + 964 = _____

2   34,573 − 1,255 = _____

3   15,465 + 23,223 = _____

4   18,247 − 11,405 = _____

Ongoing Review

5   A concert hall holds 12,655 people. 10,443 tickets were sold. How many tickets are left?

Ⓐ 2,212   Ⓑ 2,213   Ⓒ 2,222   Ⓓ 3,222

NOTE

Students practice solving addition and subtraction problems using the U.S. standard algorithms.
MWI **U.S. Standard Algorithm for Subtraction**

Using Place Value

In Problems 1–3, round each number to the nearest 10,000 and to the nearest 100,000.

	Nearest 10,000	Nearest 100,000
1 437,994		
2 603,488		
3 552,495		

In Problems 4–7, write <, >, or = in the blank to compare the two numbers.

4 379,577 _____ 365,438

5 649,121 _____ 646,889

6 400,158 _____ 401,723

7 945,942 _____ 945,878

NAME   DATE

Concert Time

The Composites are playing at a sold-out concert at the Gopherdome, which holds 40,000 people. The concert starts at 8:00 P.M. Solve these problems and record your solutions, using clear and concise notation.

1   At 7:00 P.M., 28,175 people are at the concert. How many people have not arrived yet?

2   **a.** By 7:30 P.M., 9,590 more people have arrived. How many people are at the concert now?

      b. How many people have not arrived yet?

3   By 8:00 P.M., all but 1,642 people are at the concert. How many people are at the concert now?

NOTE

Students practice solving addition and subtraction problems.
MWI Multi-Step Problems With Larger Numbers

NAME _____ DATE _____

Addition and Subtraction Problems

Solve each of the following problems. Show your work clearly.

1   9,124 + 4,279 = _____

2   8,569
         − 2,895
        ─────────

3   9,201 − 7,225 = _____

4   4,550 + 8,872 = _____

NAME

DATE

Place Value to 1,000,000

In Problems 1–4, write each number in expanded form.

1 38,956 _____

2 7,104 _____

3 648,713 _____

4 305,501 _____

In Problems 5 and 6, write $<$, $>$, or $=$ to correctly compare the two numbers.

5 42,551 _____ 40,725

6 712,726 _____ 1,000,000

NOTE

Students use place-value understanding to write numbers in expanded form and compare numbers through 1,000,000.

MWI **Place Value: Large Numbers**

Fraction Cards and Decimal Grids

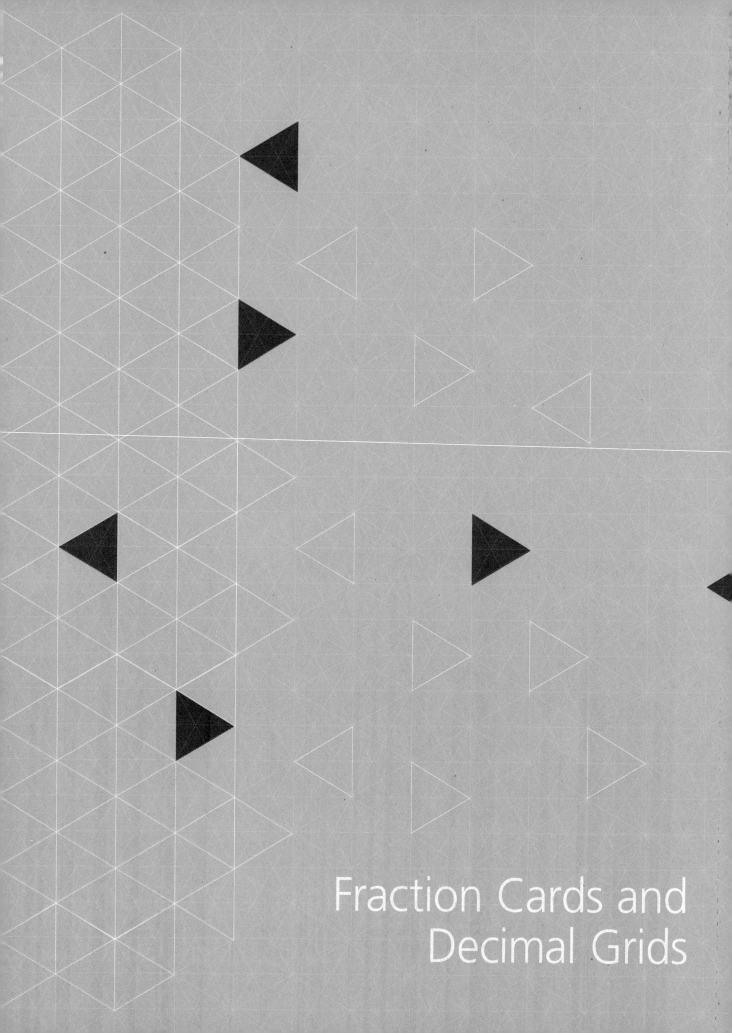

Fraction Cards and
Decimal Grids

NAME

DATE

4 × 6 Rectangles

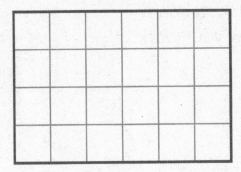

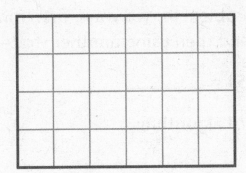

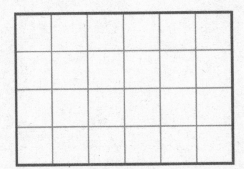

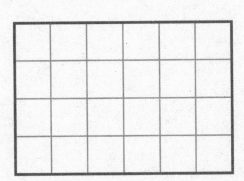

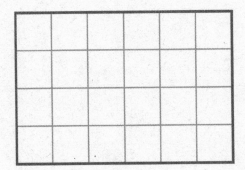

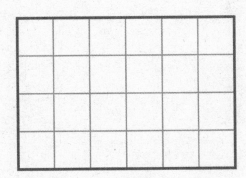

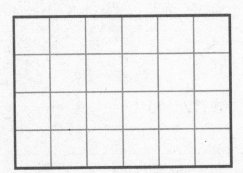

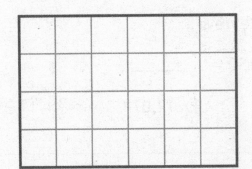

NAME   DATE

Solve Two Ways, Addition

Solve this problem in two ways, first using the U.S. standard algorithm and then using another strategy. Show your work.

$5{,}293 + 8{,}851 = $ _____

U.S. standard algorithm:

A second way:

Ongoing Review

$6{,}924 + 5{,}150 = $ _____

Ⓐ 11,024   Ⓑ 12,074   Ⓒ 11,390   Ⓓ 12,740

NOTE

Students practice strategies for solving addition problems in two different ways.
MWI Addition Strategies

NAME   DATE

Halves, Fourths, and Eighths

Shade in each fraction on one of the rectangles. Label the
fraction on each rectangle.

$\frac{1}{4}$ $\frac{1}{2}$ $\frac{2}{2}$ $\frac{3}{4}$ $\frac{1}{8}$ $\frac{7}{8}$

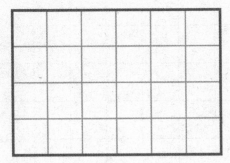   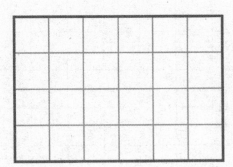

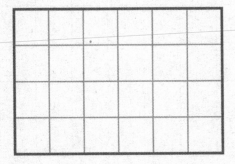   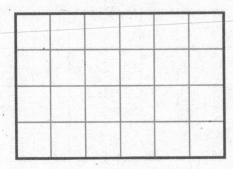

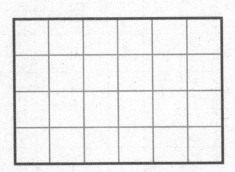   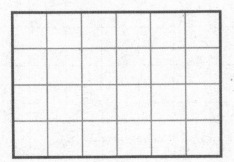

NOTE

Students represent fractions on 4 × 6 rectangles.
MWI **Fractions of an Area**

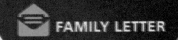
NAME   DATE

About the Mathematics in This Unit

Dear Family,

Our class is starting a new mathematics unit about fractions called *Fraction Cards and Decimal Grids.* During this unit, students represent halves, fourths, eighths, thirds, sixths, twelfths, fifths, and tenths; find equivalent fractions; and compare fractions. Students are introduced to decimal notation, represent decimals, and compare decimals. They begin computation with fractions: adding and subtracting fractions and multiplying fractions by whole numbers.

Throughout the unit, students work toward these goals:

Benchmark/Goal	Examples
Identify equivalent fractions and explain why they are equivalent.	$\frac{1}{3} = \frac{2}{6}$ *I broke the thirds in half to make sixths. There are two sixths in $\frac{1}{3}$.*
Compare fractions with like and unlike denominators.	Which is greater, $\frac{5}{6}$ or $\frac{3}{4}$? *$\frac{5}{6} > \frac{3}{4}$ because $\frac{3}{4}$ is $\frac{1}{4}$ away from 1 and $\frac{5}{6}$ is only $\frac{1}{6}$ away from 1.*
Add and subtract fractions and mixed numbers with like denominators.	Nadeem is walking to the park, which is $\frac{9}{10}$ of a mile away. He has walked $\frac{4}{10}$ of a mile. How much farther does Nadeem have to walk?
Multiply a fraction by a whole number.	Richard's recipe for chocolate chip cookies requires $\frac{1}{4}$ of a cup of sugar. He wants to make 6 batches of cookies. How much sugar does he need? $6 \times \frac{1}{4} = \underline{\hspace{1cm}}$

© Pearson Education 4

About the Mathematics in This Unit

Benchmark/Goal	Examples	
Read, write, and compare decimals in tenths and hundredths.	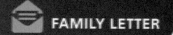	How much of the square is colored in? Decimal: $.56$ Fraction: $\dfrac{56}{100}$
Add tenths and hundredths.		$\dfrac{35}{100} + \dfrac{5}{10} = \dfrac{85}{100}$ $.35 + .5 = .85$
Represent data on a line plot including fourths and eighths.		

Butterfly Wingspans (inches)

In our math class, students spend time discussing problems in depth and are asked to share their reasoning and solutions. It is important that your child solve math problems in ways that make sense to him or her. At home, encourage your child to explain the math thinking that supports those solutions. Please look for more information and activities about *Fraction Cards and Decimal Grids* that will be sent home in the coming weeks.

NAME   DATE

Parts of Rectangles

What fraction of the rectangle is shaded? Write the fraction next to each figure.

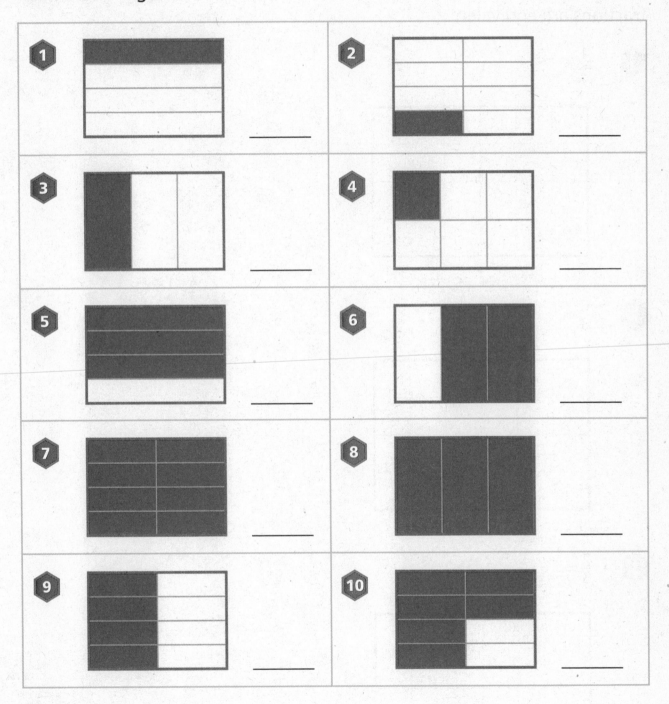

1 _____

2 _____

3 _____

4 _____

5 _____

6 _____

7 _____

8 _____

9 _____

10 _____

NOTE

Students identify fractional parts of a rectangle.
MWI **Fractional Parts**

Equivalent Fractions

Find at least one equivalent fraction for each fraction.
Show on the 4 × 6 rectangle and explain how you know the fractions are equivalent.

1 $\frac{1}{2} =$

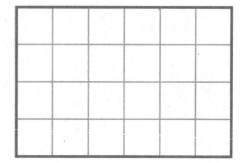

2 $\frac{6}{8} =$

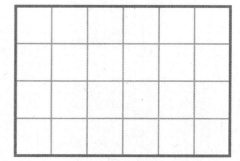

3 $\frac{2}{3} =$

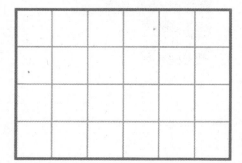

Equivalent Fractions

4 $\frac{2}{6} =$

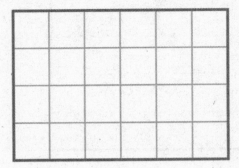

5 $\frac{3}{12} =$

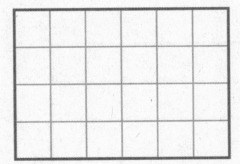

NAME

DATE

5 × 12 Rectangles

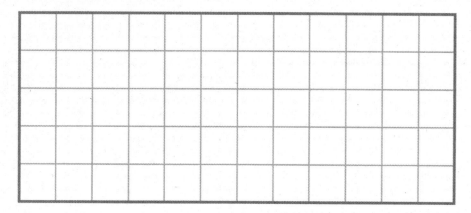

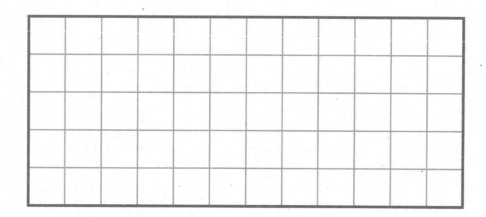

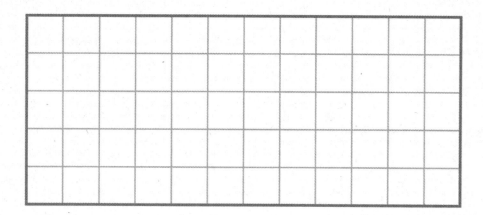

NAME

DATE

Solve Two Ways, Subtraction

Solve this problem in two ways, first using the U.S. standard algorithm and then using another strategy. Show your work.

$6,745 - 2,828 =$ _____

U.S. standard algorithm:

A second way:

Ongoing Review

$2,050 - 400 - 37 =$ _____

Ⓐ 1,023   Ⓑ 1,527   Ⓒ 1,580   Ⓓ 1,613

NOTE

Students practice strategies for solving subtraction problems in two different ways.
MWI Subtraction Strategies

NAME _____ DATE _____

Subtraction Practice

Solve each subtraction problem and show your solutions. Use the U.S. standard algorithm for at least two of the problems.

1 4,835 − 2,540 = _____

2 Jake has 773 baseball cards in his collection. Noemi has 1,215 in hers. How many more cards does Jake need to collect in order to have the same number as Noemi?

3
$$\begin{array}{r} 6,789 \\ -\ 2,199 \\ \hline \end{array}$$

4 2,205 − 1,789 = _____

NOTE

Students practice solving subtraction problems.
MWI Subtraction Strategies

NAME _____   DATE _____

Related Activities to Try at Home

Dear Family,

The activities below are related to the mathematics in the unit *Fraction Cards and Decimal Grids*. You can use the activities to enrich your child's mathematical learning experience.

Fraction and Decimal Scavenger Hunt At school, students are working on understanding fractions and decimals. Be on the lookout for examples of fractions or decimal numbers in your world—in the kitchen, in a toolbox or a sewing kit, in grocery or hardware stores, or in magazines and newspapers. Take these opportunities to talk with your child about what the fraction or decimal means.

Fair Shares You can build on the work of this unit at home by capitalizing on everyday situations that involve fractions. Issues of fairness often offer good examples of fractions.

- After making a batch of brownies and giving away part of the batch to the neighbors, you want to divide what's left equally among 3 people.
  What is $\frac{1}{3}$ of 18 brownies?
  What if you want to divide it equally among 6 people?
  What is $\frac{1}{6}$ of 18 brownies?
- Three people are sharing a pizza: $\frac{1}{3}$ has mushrooms, $\frac{1}{3}$ has pepperoni, and $\frac{1}{3}$ has onions. What might the pizza look like?

Fractions in the Kitchen Cooking is another great way to learn about fractions. Ask your child questions such as, How can we measure $\frac{3}{4}$ cup? Look together at how the fractions appear on a measuring cup. Doubling recipes or cutting them in half can help your child understand relationships such as $\frac{1}{3}$ cup $+ \frac{1}{3}$ cup $= \frac{2}{3}$ cup or $2 \times \frac{1}{3}$ cup $= \frac{2}{3}$ cup.

10 × 10 Squares

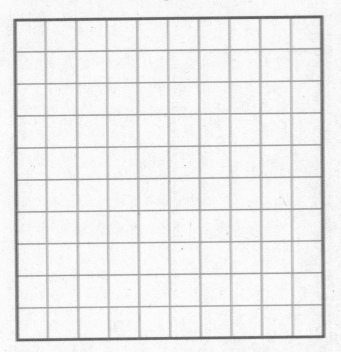

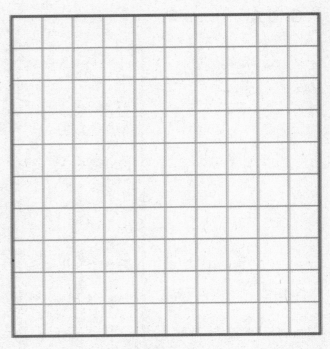

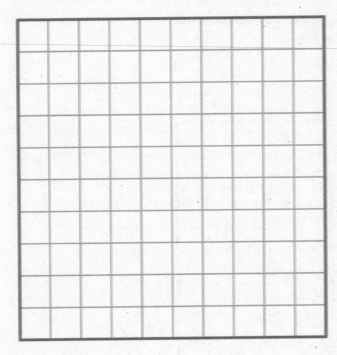

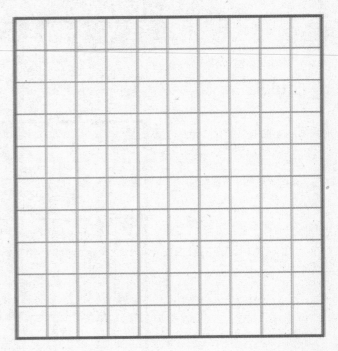

NAME

DATE

Decimal Grids A and B

Grid A

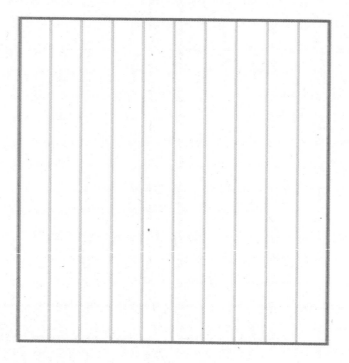

Grid B

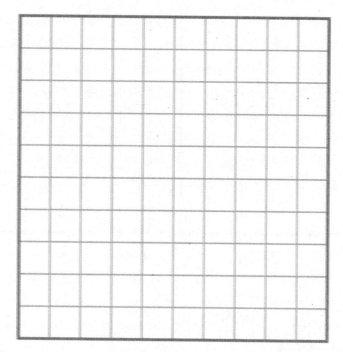

NAME _____   DATE _____

Stamp Collection

Solve these problems. Use the U.S. standard algorithm to solve at least one of them.

1 Enrique has a collection of stamps. He has 899 stamps from North America and 418 stamps from South America. If Enrique wants 1,500 stamps altogether, how many more stamps does he need?

2 Ramona also has a stamp collection. She has 941 North American stamps and 483 European stamps. If Ramona wants 1,500 stamps altogether, how many more stamps does she need?

3 Who has more stamps, Enrique or Ramona? How many more stamps?

NOTE

Students practice solving addition and subtraction problems in a story problem context.
MWI **U.S. Standard Algorithm for Subtraction**

Representing and Identifying Decimals

Each square below represents a garden. The shaded part represents the amount of the garden that is planted. In each problem you will either identify the amount planted in the garden using both fraction and decimal notation or represent the amount planted on a square.

1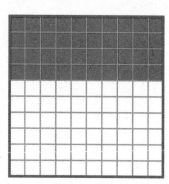

What amount of the garden was planted?

Fraction:

Decimal:

2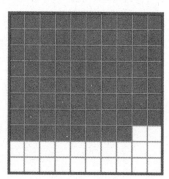

What amount of the garden was planted?

Fraction:

Decimal:

3 Sabrina planted 0.03 of her garden with tomatoes. Shade in the amount she planted.

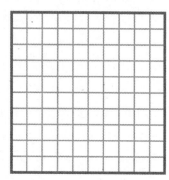

What fraction of the garden did Sabrina plant with tomatoes?

NAME   DATE

Representing and Identifying Decimals

4 Abdul planted 0.56 of his garden with lettuce.
Shade in the amount he planted with lettuce.

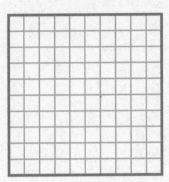

What fraction of the garden did Abdul plant with lettuce?

5

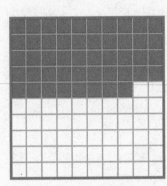

What amount of the garden was planted?

Fraction:

Decimal:

6 Noemi planted 0.2 of her garden with peas.
Shade in the amount she planted with peas.

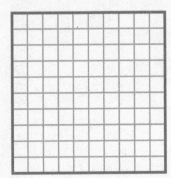

What fraction of the garden did Noemi plant with peas?

NAME

DATE

More Equivalent Fractions

Decide whether the following fractions are equivalent or not. Explain or show how you know. You can use 4×6, 5×12, or 10×10 rectangles to help you.

1   Does $\frac{3}{4} = \frac{9}{12}$?
How do you know?

2   Does $\frac{4}{6} = \frac{7}{12}$?
How do you know?

3   Does $\frac{2}{5} = \frac{4}{10}$?
How do you know?

4   Does $\frac{5}{10} = \frac{10}{100}$?
How do you know?

NAME _____   DATE _____

Addition and Subtraction Problems

Solve the problems below. Show your solutions using clear and concise notation. Use the U.S. standard algorithm for at least two of the problems.

1
$$3{,}738$$
$$-\ 689$$

2
$$4{,}515$$
$$-\ 2{,}772$$

3 $33{,}811 + 9{,}749 = $ _____

4
$$27{,}234$$
$$+\ 14{,}694$$

5 _____ $+ 1{,}349 = 8{,}250$

6 $6{,}865 - $ _____ $= 3{,}947$

NOTE

Students practice solving addition and subtraction problems.
MWI U.S. Standard Algorithm for Addition; U.S. Standard Algorithm for Subtraction

NAME

DATE

Showing Decimals on a 10 × 10 Square

Show the following decimal numbers on the squares below by shading in each amount. Each large square represents 1.

1 0.7

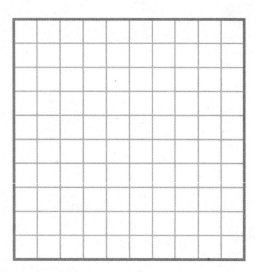

2 0.75

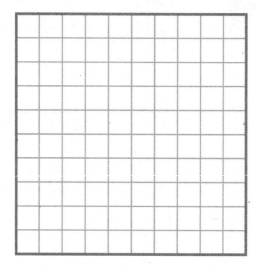

3 0.5

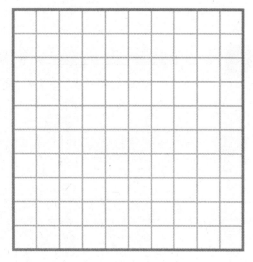

4 0.38

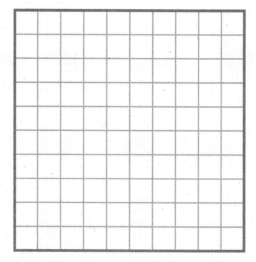

NOTE

Students shade in squares to represent decimal numbers.
MWI **Representing Decimals**

NAME

DATE

Relationship Among Equivalent Fractions

1 Does $\frac{1}{3} = \frac{2}{6}$?
Show and explain how you know. You can use
4 × 6 or 5 × 12 rectangles or draw your own
representation.

2 Does $\frac{3}{4} = \frac{6}{8}$?
Show and explain how you know. You can use
4 × 6 or 5 × 12 rectangles or draw your own
representation.

3 Does $\frac{8}{12} = \frac{2}{3}$?
Show and explain how you know. You can use
4 × 6 or 5 × 12 rectangles or draw your own
representation.

4 What do you notice about the size of the pieces and
the number of pieces in the fractions that are equivalent?

NAME DATE

What Is the Decimal?

 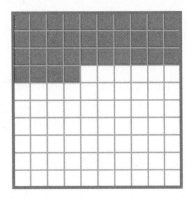

How much of the square is colored in?

Decimal:

Fraction:

 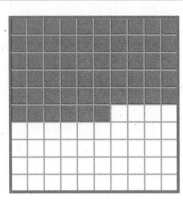

How much of the square is colored in?

Decimal:

Fraction:

 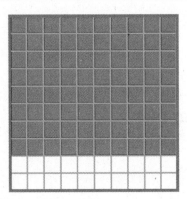

How much of the square is colored in?

Decimal:

Fraction:

 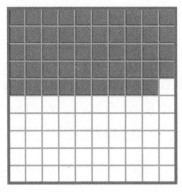

How much of the square is colored in?

Decimal:

Fraction:

NOTE

Students identify the portions of squares that are shaded in and name the portions with decimals and fractions.
MWI **Representing Decimals**

NAME

DATE

Fractions for Fraction Cards

$1\frac{3}{4}$	$\frac{1}{2}$	$1\frac{1}{2}$	$1\frac{1}{3}$
$\frac{4}{5}$	$1\frac{1}{4}$	$\frac{6}{8}$	$\frac{3}{6}$
$\frac{5}{3}$	$\frac{2}{4}$	$\frac{2}{6}$	$\frac{0}{4}$
$\frac{9}{4}$	$\frac{8}{6}$	$\frac{1}{4}$	$\frac{5}{4}$
$\frac{5}{6}$	$\frac{2}{5}$	$\frac{3}{12}$	$\frac{6}{3}$
$\frac{7}{8}$	$\frac{4}{10}$	$\frac{1}{5}$	$\frac{8}{12}$
$\frac{0}{2}$	$2\frac{1}{2}$	$\frac{8}{8}$	$\frac{3}{2}$
$\frac{2}{12}$	$\frac{1}{3}$	$\frac{9}{6}$	$\frac{2}{3}$
$\frac{1}{6}$	$\frac{3}{3}$	$\frac{4}{2}$	$\frac{1}{8}$
$\frac{5}{2}$	$\frac{3}{8}$	$\frac{3}{4}$	$\frac{4}{3}$

NAME

DATE

How Many Miles?

The Kwan family is taking a trip across the United States. They started in New York, drove to California, and are driving back. Solve the following problems about their mileage and explain how you found the difference between the numbers.

1 On July 1, they have gone 425 miles. How many more miles until they have gone 1,000 miles?

2 On July 5, they have gone 620 miles. How many more miles until they have gone 2,000 miles?

3 On July 20, they have gone 1,495 miles. How many more miles until they have gone 3,000 miles?

4 On August 1, they are on their way back to New York. They have gone 4,690 miles. Their total trip will be about 6,000 miles. How many more miles do they still have to drive?

Ongoing Review

5 $5,010 -$ _____ $= 4,880$

Ⓐ 30 Ⓑ 50 Ⓒ 130 Ⓓ 220

NOTE

Students use addition and subtraction to solve problems about distances in miles.
MWI Addition Strategies

NAME   DATE

Are These Fractions Equivalent?

Decide whether the following fractions are equivalent or not.
Explain or show how you know. You can use the rectangles to
help you.

1 Does $\frac{2}{3} = \frac{8}{12}$?
How do you know?

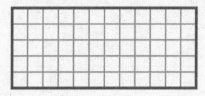

2 Does $\frac{2}{6} = \frac{5}{12}$?
How do you know?

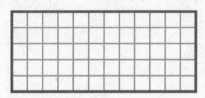

3 Does $\frac{3}{6} = \frac{5}{8}$?
How do you know?

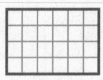

4 Does $\frac{4}{10} = \frac{2}{5}$?
How do you know?

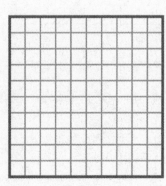

NOTE

Students decide if a pair of fractions are equivalent and show their reasoning.
MWI **Generating Equivalent Fractions**

NAME

DATE

What's the Fraction?

1 Here are pictures of some Fraction Cards. On each one, write the name of the shaded fraction that is shown.

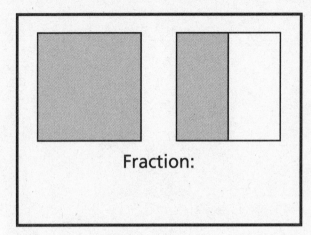

Fraction:

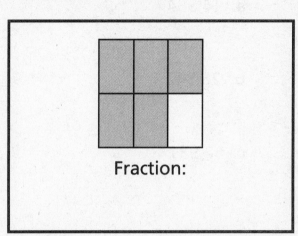

Fraction:

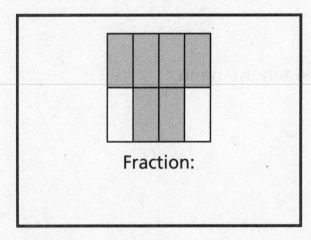

Fraction:

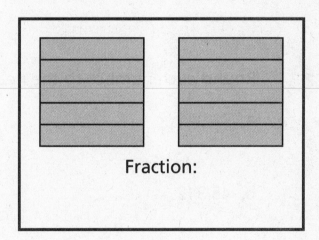

Fraction:

2 Choose one of the fractions above and draw a picture of an equivalent fraction.

3 How do you know these two fractions are equivalent? Write in the space below or on another sheet of paper.

NAME

DATE

Expanded Form and Rounding Numbers

1 Write the following numbers in expanded notation.

    a. 14,984

    b. 26,342

    c. 52,931

2 Round each number to the nearest ten thousand.

    a. 72,941

    b. 45,312

    c. 86,235

NOTE

Students write numbers in expanded form and round numbers to the nearest ten thousand.

MWI **Rounding Large Numbers**

Finding Equivalent Fractions

As you are playing *Capture Fractions,* keep track of the matches you make by writing equations that show equivalent fractions.

Example: $\frac{1}{2} = \frac{4}{8}$

I found these equivalent fractions:

NAME   DATE

Reading a Long Book

Solve these problems. Show your work.

1 Yuki is reading a book that is 1,200 pages long. So far, he has read 189 pages. How many more pages does he have to read to finish the book?

2 Over the next three weeks, Yuki reads 342 more pages. How many pages has he read so far?

3 At the end of six weeks, Yuki has read 977 pages. How many more pages does he have left to finish the book?

Ongoing Review

4 How many tens are there in 3,102?

Ⓐ 31   Ⓑ 310   Ⓒ 3,100   Ⓓ 3,102

NOTE

Students practice solving addition and subtraction problems in a story problem context.
MWI Subtraction Strategies

NAME _____   DATE _____

Which Is Greater?

Which is greater, $\frac{2}{3}$ or $\frac{3}{2}$? Use words and pictures to explain your answer.

NOTE

Students compare a pair of fractions.

 **Fractional Parts**

NAME _____ DATE _____

Fractions in Containers

Write each fraction below the container in which it belongs.
Cross out each fraction as you use it. $\left(\frac{3}{6}\text{ has been done for you.}\right)$

There are five fractions for each container.

$\frac{3}{6}$ $\frac{5}{5}$ $\frac{1}{4}$ $\frac{5}{2}$ $\frac{1}{5}$ $\frac{2}{3}$ $\frac{2}{2}$ $\frac{3}{5}$ $\frac{5}{8}$ $\frac{6}{3}$ $\frac{2}{5}$ $\frac{2}{4}$ $\frac{3}{3}$

$\frac{5}{10}$ $\frac{3}{10}$ $\frac{10}{5}$ $\frac{2}{6}$ $\frac{3}{2}$ $\frac{9}{10}$ $\frac{6}{5}$ $\frac{10}{10}$ $\frac{4}{8}$ $\frac{4}{5}$ $\frac{8}{8}$ $\frac{6}{12}$

Less than one half	One half	Between one half and one whole	One whole	More than one whole
	$\frac{3}{6}$			

NAME _____ DATE _____

Addition and Subtraction Practice

Solve the following problems using the U.S. standard algorithms.

1   34,500 + 964 = _____

2   34,500 − 1,255 = _____

3   15,465 + 3,223 = _____

Ongoing Review

4   A concert hall holds 12,655 people. 10,443 tickets were sold. How many tickets are left?

Ⓐ 2,212   Ⓑ 2,213   Ⓒ 2,222   Ⓓ 3,222

NOTE

Students solve addition and subtraction problems.
MWI U.S. Standard Algorithm for Addition; U.S. Standard Algorithm for Subtraction

© Pearson Education **4**

NAME _____ DATE _____

Fraction Number Line

Spread out your Landmark Cards $\left(0, \frac{1}{2}, 1, \text{ and } 2\right)$. Order half of your group's deck of Fraction Cards from least to greatest, placing the cards on top of and in between your Landmark Cards. Record where you place each fraction on the number line below.

NAME   DATE

Subtracting Numbers in the Thousands

Solve each problem below in two ways. Use the U.S. standard algorithm as one way, and choose another strategy for the second way.

1 7,249 − 4,832 = _____

U.S. standard algorithm: A second way:

2 16,207 − 8,112 = _____

U.S. standard algorithm: A second way:

 3
    21,462
−   8,993

U.S. standard algorithm: A second way:

NOTE

Students practice solving subtraction problems with larger numbers.

MWI **U.S. Standard Algorithm for Subtraction**

Fill-In Fractions

Fill in the box for each fraction so that it represents the amount stated for each box. The first fraction has been done for you.

1 Less than $\frac{1}{2}$

$\frac{3}{8}$ $\frac{3}{\boxed{}}$ $\frac{\boxed{}}{5}$

2 $\frac{1}{2}$

$\frac{\boxed{}}{4}$ $\frac{5}{\boxed{}}$ $\frac{\boxed{}}{12}$

3 Between $\frac{1}{2}$ and 1

$\frac{2}{\boxed{}}$ $\frac{\boxed{}}{6}$ $\frac{3}{\boxed{}}$

4 1

$\frac{\boxed{}}{3}$ $\frac{\boxed{}}{8}$ $\frac{2}{\boxed{}}$

5 Between 1 and $1\frac{1}{2}$

$\frac{\boxed{}}{8}$ $\frac{6}{\boxed{}}$ $\frac{5}{\boxed{}}$

6 More than $1\frac{1}{2}$

$\frac{5}{\boxed{}}$ $\frac{\boxed{}}{3}$ $\frac{4}{\boxed{}}$

NOTE

Students write fractions that are equal to or between landmarks.
MWI Fractional Parts

© Pearson Education 4

NAME _____   DATE _____

Make Your Move

The fractions on each clothesline are out of order. Show how to fix the order with just one move.

  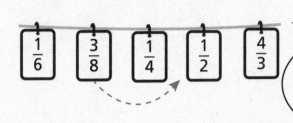

I need to move the $\frac{3}{8}$. $\frac{1}{4}$ is the same as $\frac{2}{8}$, and $\frac{1}{2}$ is the same as $\frac{4}{8}$. So $\frac{3}{8}$ should go between them.

2 | $\frac{1}{8}$ | $\frac{1}{4}$ | $\frac{2}{3}$ | $\frac{1}{2}$ | $\frac{4}{4}$ |

3 | $\frac{1}{6}$ | $\frac{1}{8}$ | $\frac{1}{4}$ | $\frac{1}{3}$ | $\frac{3}{4}$ |

4 | $\frac{1}{5}$ | $\frac{1}{3}$ | $\frac{1}{2}$ | $\frac{7}{8}$ | $\frac{5}{8}$ |

5 | $\frac{3}{10}$ | $\frac{3}{8}$ | $\frac{3}{4}$ | $\frac{3}{6}$ | $\frac{3}{2}$ |

Ongoing Review

6 Which total is **less than** 100?

Ⓐ 44 + 54   Ⓑ 53 + 57   Ⓒ 81 + 20   Ⓓ 76 + 24

NOTE

Students put fractions in the correct order.
MWI **Comparing Fractions**

Decimals for Decimal Cards

0.1	0.25
0.45	0.75
0.5	1.25
0.95	0.2
0.8	0.9

Selling Fruit

Solve these problems. Show your work on a separate sheet of paper.

1 On Monday, a grocery store received a shipment of 2,700 peaches. The store sold 567 of them that day. How many peaches were left to sell the next day?

2 On Wednesday, the store received a shipment of 3,850 grapefruits. The store sold 362 grapefruits that day. How many grapefruits were left to sell the next day?

3 On Saturday, the store received a shipment of 1,500 melons. The store sold 734 melons on Saturday and 674 melons on Sunday. How many melons were left to sell on Monday morning?

Ongoing Review

4 Which number is three tenths?

Ⓐ 0.03 Ⓑ 0.3 Ⓒ 3.0 Ⓓ 3.10

NOTE

Students practice solving addition and subtraction problems in a story problem context.
MWI Subtraction Problem Types

NAME _____ DATE _____

Comparing Decimals

Place a symbol (< or >) in the box to compare the decimals.
You can use the 10 × 10 squares to help you.

1   0.37 ☐ 0.4

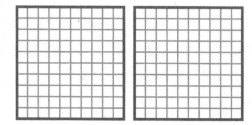

2   0.9 ☐ 0.74

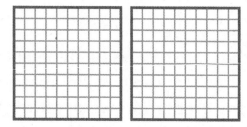

3   0.91 ☐ 0.53

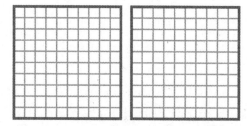

4   0.46 ☐ 0.7

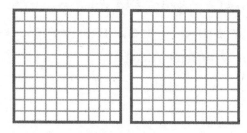

5   0.65 ☐ 0.82

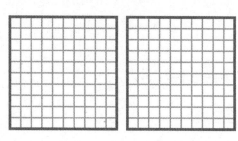

NOTE

Students decide which of two decimals is greater.
MWI Comparing Decimals

NAME

DATE

Showing Decimals on a 10 × 10 Square

Show the following decimal numbers on the squares below by shading in each amount. Each large square represents 1.

1 0.1

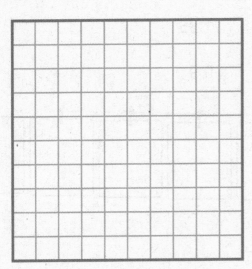

2 0.45

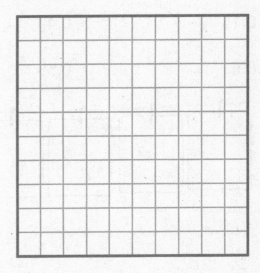

3 0.6

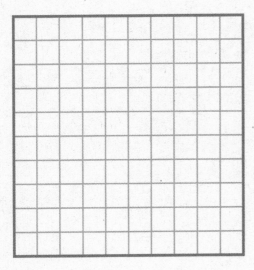

4 0.95

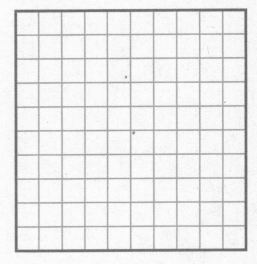

NOTE

Students represent decimals on a square that represents 1.

MWI Representing Decimals

© Pearson Education 4

NAME _____ DATE _____

Ordering Decimals

Put these decimals in order from least to greatest. Use the clothesline below to order them.

0.85	0.35	1.2
0.15	0.4	1.35
0.6	0.55	0.9

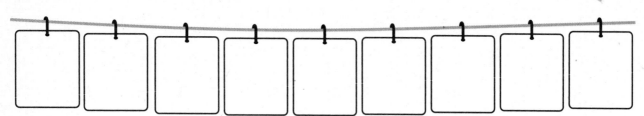

NOTE

Students put decimals in order from least to greatest.
MWI **Comparing Decimals**

Decomposing Fractions

Show all the ways you can think of to make each fraction using other fractions. Write each way using an addition equation.

 $\frac{7}{8}$

Example: $\frac{1}{8} + \frac{3}{8} + \frac{3}{8} = \frac{7}{8}$

 $\frac{5}{6}$

© Pearson Education 4

Adding Fractions

Solve each problem and show your solution. Write an equation.

1   Richard needs $\frac{2}{4}$ cup of flour for the cookies he is making. He needs $\frac{3}{4}$ cup of flour for the muffins he is making. How much flour does he need?

2   It is $\frac{5}{6}$ of a mile from Yuki's house to his school. It is $\frac{2}{6}$ of a mile further from Yuki's school to the library. How far is it from Yuki's house to the library?

3   On Monday Amelia ate $\frac{2}{5}$ of the bag of apples she bought. On Tuesday she ate another $\frac{1}{5}$ of the bag of apples she bought. What fraction of the bag of apples did she eat altogether?

4   Anna ate $\frac{1}{2}$ of a sandwich. Damian ate another $\frac{1}{4}$ of the same sandwich. How much of the sandwich did they eat in all?

Adding Fractions

Solve each problem and show your solution.

5 $\frac{4}{8} + \frac{3}{8} =$ _____

6 $\frac{1}{3} + \frac{2}{3} + \frac{2}{3} =$ _____

7 $\frac{1}{2} + \frac{3}{6} + \frac{4}{8} =$ _____

8 $\frac{3}{12} + \frac{1}{12} + \frac{5}{12} =$ _____

9 $\frac{1}{3} + \frac{2}{6} =$ _____

10 $\frac{6}{10} + \frac{7}{10} =$ _____

NAME _____ DATE _____

More Adding Fractions

Solve each problem and show your solution.

1 $\frac{3}{8} + \frac{2}{8} =$ _____

2 $\frac{2}{6} + \frac{5}{6} =$ _____

3 Derek ate $\frac{3}{4}$ of a pizza. Luke ate $\frac{1}{4}$ of a pizza. How much pizza did they eat altogether?

4 $\frac{4}{10} + \frac{3}{10} + \frac{11}{10} =$ _____

5 $\frac{3}{12} + \frac{6}{12} =$ _____

NOTE

Students add fractions with like denominators.

MWI Adding Fractions With Like Denominators

NAME

DATE

More Decomposing Fractions

Show all the ways you can think of to make each fraction using other fractions. Write each way using an addition equation.

1 $\frac{3}{5}$

2 $\frac{11}{12}$

NOTE

Students decompose fractions.
MWI **Fractional Parts**

Subtracting Fractions

Solve each problem and show your work. For the word problems, write an equation.

1 There was $\frac{7}{8}$ of a pan of brownies on the table. Some friends came over and ate $\frac{4}{8}$ of the pan of brownies. What fraction of the pan of brownies is left?

2 Marisol lives $\frac{6}{10}$ of a mile from her school. She has already walked $\frac{4}{10}$ of a mile. How much farther does Marisol have to walk to get to school?

3 There was $\frac{7}{12}$ of a gallon of milk in the refrigerator. The Jones family used some of the milk during breakfast. There is $\frac{3}{12}$ of a gallon of milk left. How much milk did the Jones family use during breakfast?

4 $\frac{4}{5} - \frac{2}{5} =$ _____

5 $\frac{9}{12} - \frac{5}{12} =$ _____

More Subtracting Fractions

Solve each problem and show your work. For the word problems, write an equation.

1 There was $\frac{7}{8}$ of a carton of juice in the refrigerator. The Ortega family drank $\frac{5}{8}$ of the carton with their breakfast. What fraction of the carton remains?

2 Venetta lives $\frac{3}{4}$ of a mile away from the library. Anna lives $\frac{1}{4}$ of a mile away from the library. How much farther from the library does Venetta live than Anna?

3 Richard had $\frac{4}{5}$ of a bag of carrots. He fed $\frac{2}{5}$ of the bag to his rabbit. What fraction of the bag did Richard have left?

4 $\frac{7}{10} - \frac{4}{10} =$ _____

5 $\frac{6}{8} - \frac{1}{8} =$ _____

NOTE

Students solve subtraction problems involving fractions with like denominators.

MWI Subtracting Fractions With Like Denominators

Butterfly Wingspans

Yuki went to the Natural History Museum to study butterflies. The information he has about some of the butterflies in the collection is shown below.

Name	Wingspan (inches)	Name	Wingspan (inches)
American Snout	$1\frac{1}{2}$	Pearl Crescent	$1\frac{5}{8}$
Giant Swallowtail	$5\frac{1}{4}$	Postman	$2\frac{1}{2}$
Julia	$3\frac{1}{2}$	Red Admiral	$3\frac{1}{8}$
Milbert's Tortoiseshell	$2\frac{5}{8}$	Saturn	$4\frac{1}{4}$
Monarch	$3\frac{1}{2}$	Tiger Swallowtail	$3\frac{3}{4}$
Painted Lady	$2\frac{1}{2}$	Viceroy	$2\frac{7}{8}$

Record the measurements on the line plot below.

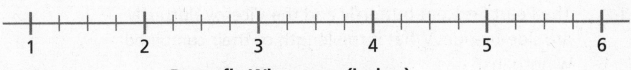

Butterfly Wingspans (inches)

Write three statements that describe the data.

© Pearson Education **4**

Butterfly Wingspans

Use the information on the previous page to solve the following problems. Show your work.

1 How much longer is the wingspan of the Viceroy butterfly than the wingspan of the Pearl Crescent butterfly?

2 How much longer is the wingspan of the Giant Swallowtail butterfly than the wingspan of the Tiger Swallowtail butterfly?

3 The American Snout butterfly and the Postman butterfly are side-by-side. What is the length of their combined wingspans?

4 How much longer is the wingspan of the Red Admiral butterfly than the wingspan of the Milbert's Tortoiseshell butterfly?

5 The Pearl Crescent butterfly and the Viceroy butterfly are side-by-side. What is the length of their combined wingspans?

6 The Saturn butterfly and the Tiger Swallowtail butterfly are side-by-side. What is the length of their combined wingspans?

© Pearson Education **4**

NAME   DATE

Fraction Subtraction

Solve each problem and show your work. For the word problems, write an equation.

1 There was $\frac{5}{6}$ of a pot of soup on the stove. The Kim family ate some of the soup. $\frac{4}{6}$ of the pot of soup is left. What fraction of the pot of soup did the Kim family eat?

2 Nadeem is walking to the park, which is $\frac{9}{10}$ of a mile away. He has walked $\frac{4}{10}$ of a mile. How much farther does Nadeem have to walk?

3 Tonya had $\frac{10}{12}$ of a yard of fabric. She used $\frac{5}{12}$ of a yard of fabric to make a lampshade. What fraction of a yard of fabric is left?

4 $\frac{7}{8} - \frac{2}{8} = $ _____

5 $\frac{3}{5} - \frac{1}{5} = $ _____

NOTE

Students solve subtraction problems involving fractions with like denominators.
MWI Subtracting Fractions With Like Denominators

NAME   DATE

Pepper's Puppies

Cheyenne's dog, Pepper, had puppies. Cheyenne recorded their weights on the line plot below.

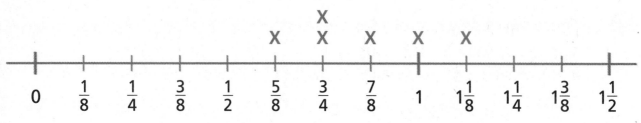

Weights of Pepper's Puppies (pounds)

Solve each problem and show your work.

1   Two puppies weighed the same amount. What was the total weight of the two puppies?

2   How much more did the heaviest puppy weigh than the lightest puppy?

3   The heaviest puppy gained $\frac{4}{8}$ of a pound in its first month. How much did it weigh after the first month?

NOTE

Students solve addition and subtraction problems involving fractions and mixed numbers using data given on a line plot.

MWI Adding and Subtracting Mixed Numbers

Adding and Subtracting Fractions and Mixed Numbers

Solve each problem and show how you solved the problem.

1 Benson had $\frac{7}{8}$ of a pound of sugar. He used some of the sugar to make muffins. He has $\frac{3}{8}$ of a pound of sugar left. How much sugar did he use to make muffins?

2 Venetta is filling up her fish tank that can hold 10 gallons of water. The fish tank has $1\frac{2}{3}$ gallons of water in it already. She adds $3\frac{2}{3}$ gallons of water to it. How many more gallons of water can be added to it?

3 $\frac{11}{6} - \frac{5}{6} =$ _____

4 $\frac{4}{5} + \frac{3}{5} =$ _____

Adding and Subtracting Fractions and Mixed Numbers

5 The cooks at Green Bean Restaurant bought 10 bags of potatoes. On Monday the cooks used $2\frac{3}{4}$ bags of potatoes. On Tuesday they used $1\frac{3}{4}$ bags of potatoes. On Wednesday they used $3\frac{1}{4}$ bags of potatoes. How many bags of potatoes do they have left?

6 After school, Abdul spent $\frac{3}{2}$ hours on homework, $\frac{3}{2}$ hours playing soccer, and $\frac{1}{2}$ of an hour reading. How much time did he spend on these after-school activities?

7 Terrell walks $\frac{4}{10}$ of a mile to school. Noemi walks $\frac{9}{10}$ of a mile to school. How much farther does Noemi walk to school?

8 $6\frac{5}{8} - 2\frac{7}{8} = $ _____

NAME   DATE

More Adding and Subtracting Fractions and Mixed Numbers

Solve each problem and show how you solved the problem.

1 On Tuesday, Amelia used $5\frac{1}{5}$ pounds of flour. On Wednesday, she used $2\frac{3}{5}$ pounds of flour. Amelia started with 10 pounds of flour. How much does she have left?

2 Enrique lives $5\frac{3}{8}$ miles from school. Jill lives $2\frac{2}{8}$ miles further from school than Enrique. How far does Jill live from school?

3 $\frac{11}{12} - \frac{4}{12} =$ _____

4 $\frac{5}{8} + \frac{6}{8} =$ _____

NOTE

Students solve word problems involving addition and subtraction of fractions or mixed numbers.

MWI Adding and Subtracting Mixed Numbers

Lizard Lengths

Enrique went to the Natural History Museum to study lizards. The information he gathered about some of the lizards in the collection is shown below.

Name	Length (feet)	Name	Length (feet)
Bearded Dragon	$1\frac{1}{2}$	Green Iguana	$4\frac{3}{4}$
Crocodile Monitor	$5\frac{3}{4}$	Mongrove Monitor	$3\frac{1}{4}$
Leopard Gecko	$\frac{3}{4}$	Panther Chameleon	$4\frac{1}{2}$
Rhinoceros Iguana	$3\frac{3}{4}$	Tuatara Lizard	$1\frac{3}{4}$
Frilled Lizard	$2\frac{3}{4}$	Argus Monitor	$3\frac{1}{2}$
Nile Monitor	$4\frac{1}{4}$	Green Water Dragon	$2\frac{1}{4}$

Record the measurements on the line plot below.

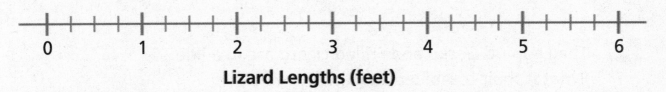

Lizard Lengths (feet)

On a separate sheet of paper, write three statements that describe the data.

NOTE

Students record measurement data involving fractions and mixed numbers on a line plot and solve problems about the data on the line plot.
MWI **Working With Data**

Lizard Lengths

Use the information on the previous page to solve the following problems. Show your work.

1 How much longer is the Crocodile Monitor than the Panther Chameleon?

2 How much longer is the Mongrove Monitor than the Green Water Dragon?

3 The Rhinoceros Iguana and the Bearded Dragon are in a line. What is their combined length?

4 How much longer is the Argus Monitor than the Tuatara Lizard?

5 The Leopard Gecko and Frilled Lizard are in a line. What is their combined length?

6 The Green Iguana and the Nile Monitor are in a line. What is their combined length?

Runner's Log

Derek made a log of how many miles he ran during a week.

Day	Mileage	Comments
Monday	2.2 miles	I ran around the pond once.
Tuesday	1.5 miles	I ran on the track, six times around.
Wednesday	1.25 miles	I ran on the track again.
Thursday	0 miles	I was tired and took the day off.
Friday	2.9 miles	I was visiting my aunt and ran with her.
Saturday	0.8 mile	I was worn out from yesterday.
Sunday	1 mile	I ran pretty slowly.

1 How far did Derek run this week?

2 Show how you figured it out.

Runner's Log

Lucy: $9\frac{1}{2}$ years old; has run two races before

Day	Mileage	Comments
Monday	1.75 miles	I ran with my mom to the store, but we got a ride back.
Tuesday	1.6 miles	Jamie and I ran to school because we were late!
Wednesday	0 miles	I had to do chores today, so I could not run.
Thursday	3.2 miles	I ran slowly, but much farther than before.
Friday	0.5 mile	I was really tired, so I only ran around the track twice.
Saturday	1.75 miles	I ran home from the store, but slowly.
Sunday	0.8 mile	I ran pretty fast, but not very far.

3   How many miles did Lucy run?

4   Show how you figured it out.

NAME

DATE

Bug Collections

The science class collected crickets and beetles. The students made line plots to show the lengths of the insects.

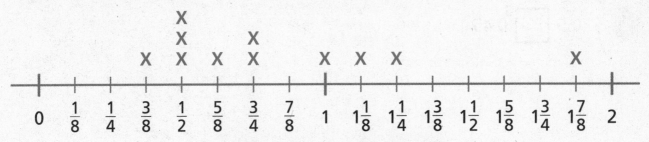

Lengths of Crickets (inches)

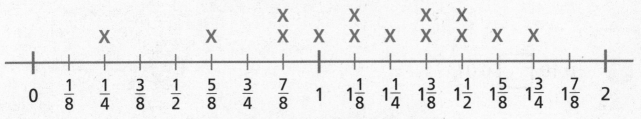

Lengths of Beetles (inches)

1 How much longer is the longest cricket than the shortest cricket?

2 How much longer is the longest beetle than the shortest beetle?

3 The cricket Benson found is $1\frac{1}{8}$ inches long. How much longer is this cricket than the shortest one in the collection?

4 $\frac{5}{8} + \frac{6}{8} =$ _____

NOTE

Students solve addition and subtraction problems involving fractions using data given on a line plot.
MWI Adding and Subtracting Mixed Numbers

© Pearson Education 4

NAME

DATE

Which Is More?

Place a symbol (< or >) in the box to compare the decimals.
Explain how you figured out which is more.

1   0.5 ☐ 0.45

2   0.10 ☐ 0.01

3   0.05 ☐ 0.5

NOTE

Students work with and compare some common decimals in order to decide which number is greater.

MWI Comparing Decimals

NAME

DATE

Comparing Fractions

Place a symbol ($<$, $>$, $=$) in the box to compare the fractions.

1 $\dfrac{1}{3}$ ☐ $\dfrac{3}{5}$ **2** $\dfrac{5}{6}$ ☐ $\dfrac{2}{3}$

3 $\dfrac{1}{2}$ ☐ $\dfrac{1}{8}$ **4** $\dfrac{6}{10}$ ☐ $\dfrac{3}{5}$

5 $\dfrac{4}{5}$ ☐ $\dfrac{1}{2}$ **6** $\dfrac{7}{10}$ ☐ $\dfrac{1}{4}$

7 $\dfrac{3}{8}$ ☐ $\dfrac{5}{8}$ **8** $\dfrac{2}{3}$ ☐ $\dfrac{3}{4}$

9 $\dfrac{1}{4}$ ☐ $\dfrac{2}{8}$ **10** $\dfrac{4}{8}$ ☐ $\dfrac{3}{5}$

11 $\dfrac{9}{10}$ ☐ $\dfrac{4}{5}$ **12** $\dfrac{2}{8}$ ☐ $\dfrac{1}{3}$

Ongoing Review

13   Which shows the fractions in order from least to greatest?

   Ⓐ $\dfrac{1}{2}, \dfrac{3}{8}, \dfrac{1}{6}$ Ⓒ $\dfrac{3}{8}, \dfrac{1}{2}, \dfrac{1}{6}$

   Ⓑ $\dfrac{1}{6}, \dfrac{3}{8}, \dfrac{1}{2}$ Ⓓ $\dfrac{1}{6}, \dfrac{1}{2}, \dfrac{3}{8}$

NOTE

Students determine which is the greater fraction in each pair.
MWI Fractional Parts

NAME

DATE

Adding Tenths and Hundredths

Solve each problem. Use the 10 × 10 squares to show your work.

1 $\frac{24}{100} + \frac{5}{10} =$ —————

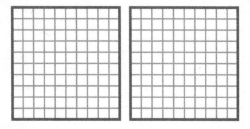

2 $\frac{52}{100} + \frac{65}{100} =$ —————

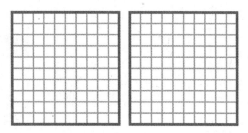

3 $\frac{8}{10} + \frac{48}{100} =$ —————

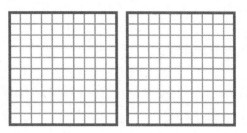

NOTE

Students represent and add tenths and hundredths.
MWI **Adding Tenths and Hundredths**

ACTIVITY

Multiplying Fractions by Whole Numbers

Use a representation to solve each problem. For each word problem, write a multiplication equation that represents the problem.

1 Jake bought three kinds of pizza for a party. Each pizza was the same size. By the end of the party $\frac{3}{4}$ of each pizza was eaten. How much pizza was eaten in all?

2 A class is counting by $\frac{2}{6}$s. What number does the 7th person say?

3 Amelia ran $\frac{2}{3}$ of a mile each day for 5 days. How far did she run total?

© Pearson Education 4

Multiplying Fractions by Whole Numbers

4 $6 \times \dfrac{1}{3} =$ _____

5 $3 \times \dfrac{3}{8} =$ _____

6   Richard's recipe for chocolate chip cookies requires $\dfrac{1}{4}$ cup of sugar. He wants to make 6 batches of cookies. How much sugar does he need?

NAME _____ DATE _____

Chunks of Cheese

Morris Mouse's Cheese House sells chunks of cheese. Each chunk weighs $\frac{3}{4}$ of a pound. Find the total weight of each kind of cheese. Use a representation to solve each problem. Also, write a multiplication equation that represents the problem. Show your work.

1 5 chunks of cheddar cheese

Total weight _____

2 10 chunks of Swiss cheese

Total weight _____

3 4 chunks of American cheese

Total weight _____

4 8 chunks of Parmesan cheese

Total weight _____

NOTE

Students solve problems involving multiplication of a whole number and a fraction.
MWI Multiplying Fractions by Whole Numbers

UNIT 6 | **413** | SESSION 4.1   © Pearson Education 4

NAME
DATE

Multiplying Fractions

Solve each problem and show your solution.

1 Mr. Stein bikes to work. The round trip distance he bikes each day is $\frac{7}{8}$ of a mile. What is the total distance he bikes in 5 days?

2 Each week, Sabrina's cat eats $\frac{4}{5}$ of a bag of cat food. How many bags of cat food does her cat eat in 7 weeks?

3 $9 \times \frac{6}{8} = $ _____

4 $5 \times \frac{8}{12} = $ _____

NOTE

Students solve problems involving multiplication of fractions and whole numbers.
MWI Multiplying Fractions by Whole Numbers

UNIT 6 | **414** | SESSION 4.1   © Pearson Education 4

More Multiplying Fractions by Whole Numbers

Use a representation to solve each problem. For each word problem, write a multiplication equation that represents the problem.

1 Sabrina walks to school every morning. Her house is $\frac{3}{8}$ of a mile from school. How many miles would she walk to school in 5 days?

2 $6 \times \frac{2}{5} =$ _____

3 Damian has a recipe that calls for $\frac{2}{3}$ of a cup of flour. He wants to make 4 times the recipe. How much flour does he need?

More Multiplying Fractions by Whole Numbers

4 $3 \times \frac{3}{4} =$ _____

5 In the store Damian found pretzels that came in $\frac{1}{3}$-pound bags. He bought 5 bags of pretzels. How many pounds of pretzels did he buy?

6 $3 \times \frac{6}{8} =$ _____

Fraction Word Problems

Solve each problem and show how you solved it.

1 Jill used stones that were each $\frac{3}{4}$ of a foot high to build a wall. She piled 6 stones on top of each other. How many feet high was her wall?

2 Anna worked for $\frac{5}{6}$ of an hour in the garden. She dug up her garden for $\frac{3}{6}$ of an hour, planted seeds for $\frac{1}{6}$ of an hour, and watered the garden for the rest of the time. For what fraction of an hour did Anna water the garden?

3 Yuki was making costumes for a play. She needed $\frac{7}{8}$ of a yard of orange fabric for one costume and $1\frac{3}{8}$ yards of orange fabric for the other costume. How much orange fabric did she need to make the two costumes?

Fraction Word Problems

4   Bill biked $\frac{6}{10}$ of a kilometer on Monday. He biked $\frac{75}{100}$ of a kilometer on Tuesday. How far did he bike altogether on Monday and Tuesday?

5   Luke had $\frac{8}{12}$ of a carton of eggs. He used $\frac{5}{12}$ of the carton of eggs to make a quiche. He used $\frac{2}{12}$ of the carton of eggs to make a cake. What fraction of the carton of eggs does he have left?

6   An office building has 14 offices, all the same size. Steve uses $\frac{3}{4}$ of a gallon of paint to paint one office ceiling. How much paint will Steve need to paint all of the office ceilings?

NAME

DATE

Multiplying with Fractions

Use a representation to solve each problem. For the word problem, write a multiplication equation that represents the problem.

1 $4 \times \frac{1}{5} =$ _____

2 $12 \times \frac{1}{2} =$ _____

3 Helena needs 8 pieces of wire. Each piece needs to be $\frac{3}{4}$ of a foot long. What is the total length of the wire Helena needs?

NOTE

Students solve problems involving multiplication of whole numbers and fractions.
 Multiplying Fractions by Whole Numbers

NAME   DATE

More Operations with Fractions

Solve each problem and show how you solved it.

1 Ursula has a pet rabbit. Each day, the rabbit eats $\frac{3}{8}$ of a cup of carrots. How many cups of carrots does the rabbit eat over 7 days?

2 Terrell goes apple picking. He uses $\frac{3}{10}$ of his apples to make apple pie. He uses $\frac{5}{10}$ of his apples to make applesauce. What fraction of his apples does he have left?

3 Ramona has two buckets of water. One has $1\frac{3}{4}$ gallons of water in it. The other has $2\frac{3}{4}$ gallons of water in it. How much water does Ramona have in the two buckets?

NOTE

Students solve word problems involving fractions.
MWI Adding and Subtracting Mixed Numbers

NAME

DATE

All Kinds of Nuts

Use a representation to solve each problem. Also, write an equation that represents the problem.

1 Emaan bought 6 bags of walnuts. Each bag contained $\frac{3}{4}$ of a pound of walnuts. What was the total weight of the walnuts?

2 Enrique's hamster eats $\frac{2}{3}$ of a cup of nuts every week. How much nuts does Enrique need to buy to feed his hamster nuts for 4 weeks?

3 Kimberly is making 3 loaves of nut bread. For each loaf, she needs $\frac{3}{4}$ of a cup of pecans. How many cups of pecans does she need? Circle the best answer below.

between 3 and 4 cups

between 2 and 3 cups

between 1 and 2 cups

NOTE

Students solve problems involving multiplication of whole numbers and fractions.
MWI **Multiplying Fractions by Whole Numbers**

© Pearson Education 4

More Adding Tenths and Hundredths

Solve each problem and show how you solved it.

1 $\frac{3}{10} + \frac{65}{100} =$ _____

2 $\frac{45}{100} + \frac{68}{100} =$ _____

3 $\frac{51}{100} + \frac{6}{10} =$ _____

4 $\frac{32}{100} + \frac{5}{10} =$ _____

Ongoing Review

5 $\frac{36}{100} + \frac{7}{10} =$ _____

Ⓐ $1\frac{6}{100}$ Ⓑ $\frac{43}{100}$ Ⓒ $1\frac{16}{100}$ Ⓓ $\frac{43}{110}$

NOTE

Students add tenths and hundredths.

MWI Adding Tenths and Hundredths

NAME _____ DATE _____

Buying Fabric

Use a representation to solve each problem. For each word problem, write a multiplication equation that represents the problem.

1 Bill bought 6 pieces of yellow fabric. Each piece was $\frac{1}{3}$ of a yard long. How many yards of fabric did Bill buy in all?

2 Kimberly bought 2 pieces of blue fabric. Each piece was $\frac{7}{8}$ of a yard long. How many yards of fabric did Kimberly buy in all?

3 Alejandro bought 7 pieces of red fabric. Each piece was $\frac{3}{4}$ of a yard long. How many yards of fabric did Alejandro buy in all?

4 $2 \times \frac{3}{10} = $ _____

5 $9 \times \frac{1}{6} = $ _____

NOTE

Students solve problems involving multiplication of a whole number by a fraction.

MWI **Multiplying Fractions by Whole Numbers**

How Many Packages and Groups?

How Many Packages
and Groups?

Converting Measurements

In Problems 1 and 2, write the missing number in the blank.
Then complete the table.

1 1 pound = _____ ounces   **2** 1 kilogram = _____ grams

Pounds	Ounces
1	
2	
3	
4	64
5	

Kilograms	Grams
1	
2	
3	3,000
4	
5	

In Problems 3–5, convert the weights and masses.

3 13 kilograms = _____ grams

4 20 pounds = _____ ounces

5 3 pounds 9 ounces = _____ ounces

6 Which is heavier, 7 pounds or 160 ounces? How do you know?

_____

Converting Measurements

In Problems 7 and 8, write the missing number in the blank.
Then complete the table.

7 1 liter = _____ milliliters

Liters	Milliliters
1	
2	
3	
4	4,000
5	

8 1 minute = _____ seconds

Minutes	Seconds
1	
2	
3	180
4	
5	

In Problems 9–12, convert each capacity or time.

9 5 gallons = _____ quarts

10 10 pints = _____ cups

11 7 quarts = _____ pints

12 3 hours 15 minutes = _____ minutes

13 Which is longer, 190 minutes or 3 hours? Explain how you know.

_____

NAME   DATE

More Converting Measurements

Solve each riddle.

1 I am 1,000 times as big as a milliliter.
What am I? _____

2 I am 60 times as big as a minute.
What am I? _____

3 I am 1,000 times as big as a gram.
What am I? _____

Measurement Equivalents
Weight and Mass
1 pound = 16 ounces
1 kilogram = 1,000 grams
Capacity
1 gallon = 4 quarts
1 liter = 1,000 milliliters
Time
1 minute = 60 seconds
1 hour = 60 minutes

In Problems 4–9, complete each conversion.

4 8 gallons = _____ quarts

5 11 liters = _____ milliliters

6 4 kilograms = _____ grams

7 3 pounds = _____ ounces

8 7 hours = _____ minutes

9 8 minutes 14 seconds = _____ seconds

Ongoing Review

10 What is 200 more than 1,957?

Ⓐ 3,957   Ⓑ 2,157   Ⓒ 1,757   Ⓓ 2,057

NOTE

Students convert measurements from larger units to smaller units.
MWI Converting Measurement

About the Mathematics in This Unit

Dear Family,

Our class is starting a new mathematics unit about multiplication and division called *How Many Packages and Groups?*. In this unit, students build on the work they did in Unit 3. Students solve multiplication and division problems with larger numbers and share a variety of solution strategies.

Throughout the unit, students work toward these goals:

Benchmarks/Goals	Examples
Multiply two 2-digit numbers and up to a 4-digit number by a 1-digit number.	The Sunshine Fruit Company sells apples in boxes that hold 28 apples. Sam Brown ordered 32 boxes for his grocery store. How many apples does Mr. Brown have to sell? 32×28 $30 \times 20 = 600$ $2 \times 20 = 40$ $30 \times 8 = 240$ $2 \times 8 = 16$ $600 + 40 + 240 + 16 = 896$
Solve division problems with up to 4-digit dividends and 1-digit divisors.	1,004 children signed up to play in the Smith City youth basketball league. 8 children will be placed on each team. How many teams of 8 players will there be? $1,004 \div 8$ $8 \times 100 = 800$ $(1,004 - 800 = 204)$ $8 \times 20 = 160$ $(204 - 160 = 44)$ $8 \times 5 = 40$ $100 + 20 + 5 = 125$ 125 teams with 4 left over players.

About the Mathematics in This Unit

Benchmarks/Goals	Examples
Solve measurement and conversion problems.	Amelia is running a 3-kilometer race. She has run 575 meters so far. How much farther does she need to run to finish the race? (There are 1,000 meters in a kilometer.)

In our math class, students spend time discussing problems in depth and are asked to share their reasoning and solutions. It is most important that children accurately and efficiently solve math problems in ways that make sense to them. At home, encourage your child to explain his or her math thinking to you.

Please look for more information and activities about *How Many Packages and Groups?* that will be sent home in the coming weeks.

Measurement Problems

Solve each problem and show your solution.

1 The mass of a rabbit is 4 kilograms. The mass of a mouse is 45 grams. How much greater is the mass of the rabbit?

2 A chef made 5 gallons of soup. She is going to store the soup in 2-quart storage containers. How many 2-quart storage containers will she need?

3 Noemi poured 325 milliliters of water into a 3-liter pot. How much more water should be added to completely fill the pot?

4 Luke is making a cake for a wedding. The recipe calls for 3 cups of flour. He is going to make 4 times the recipe. How much flour does he need?

Measurement Problems

Write an equation for each problem with a letter standing for what you are trying to find out. Solve each problem and show how you solved it.

5 Amelia is running a 3-kilometer race. She has run 575 meters so far. How much farther does she need to run to finish the race?

6 Benson read for 2 hours and 20 minutes this week. He read the same amount each day. For how many minutes did he read each day? (Reminder: There are 7 days in a week.)

7 Mr. Dakarian bought 3 quarts of orange juice. If his family drinks 3 cups of orange juice each day, for how many days will the orange juice last?

NAME

DATE

Measurement Conversions

In Problems 1–4, write the missing number in the blank. Then complete the table.

1 1 liter = _____ milliliters

Liters	Milliliters
3	3,000
4	
5	
9	
20	

2 1 hour = _____ minutes

Hours	Minutes
4	240
5	
6	
10	
12	

3 1 kilogram = _____ grams

Kilograms	Grams
2	2,000
3	
5	
8	
15	

4 1 pound = _____ ounces

Pounds	Ounces
3	48
6	
8	128
10	
20	

NOTE

Students convert measurements from larger units to smaller units.
MWI **Converting Measurement**

NAME   DATE

More Measurement Problems

Solve each problem and show your work.

1 Marisol used $2\frac{3}{4}$ gallons of paint to paint the walls of her bedroom and $\frac{3}{4}$ of a gallon to paint the ceiling. How much paint did she use in all?

2 Jill went shopping from 3:45 P.M. to 5:00 P.M. For how long did she shop?

3 The mass of a melon is 2 kilograms. The mass of a plum is 75 grams. How much greater is the mass of the melon? (1 kilogram = 1,000 grams)

4 Bill went to the museum at 11:30 A.M. He stayed for $3\frac{1}{2}$ hours. When did he leave?

5 Terrell made 4 pints of soup. How many 2-cup servings of soup is this? (1 pint = 2 cups)

NOTE

Students use the four operations to solve problems involving measurements.
MWI **Converting Measurement**

Closest Estimate Problems

Each problem below has a choice of three estimates.
Which one do you think is closest? Circle the closest
estimate. Then write about why you think this estimate
is the closest.

1 The closest estimate for 78×7 is: 200   500   700
I think this is closest because:

2 The closest estimate for 18×26 is: 400   600   1,000
I think this is closest because:

3 The closest estimate for 32×54 is: 500   1,000   1,500
I think this is closest because:

4 Choose one or more of the problems above and solve
it to get the exact answer. Show your solution with
equations. Did you choose the closest estimate?

NAME

DATE

Stamp Collections

1 Helena has a collection of stamps. She has 734 stamps from South America and 555 stamps from Africa. How many more stamps does she need to have a total of 1,500 stamps?

2 Terrell also has a stamp collection. He has 839 stamps from Africa and 472 stamps from North America. How many more stamps does he need to have a total of 1,500 stamps?

3 How many more stamps does Terrell have in his collection than Helena has in her collection?

NOTE

Students practice solving addition and subtraction problems in a story problem context.
MWI Multi-Step Problems with Larger Numbers

NAME _____ DATE _____

More or Less?

Without actually solving each problem, decide whether the answer to each problem is more or less than the landmark numbers below each problem. Answer "yes" or "no" on the line next to each question.

1 28 × 4

More than 100? _____

More than 200? _____

2 30 × 13

More than 300? _____

More than 600? _____

3 26 × 43

More than 500? _____

More than 1,000? _____

Less than 1,500? _____

4 Choose one of the problems above and make a close estimate. Write about how you made your estimate, including what numbers you used to help you estimate.

NOTE

Students practice estimation strategies that include rounding to landmark numbers and using what they know about multiplication facts and multiplying by a multiple of 10.

MWI **Strategies for Solving Multiplication Problems**

NAME   DATE

Related Activities to Try at Home

Dear Family,

The activities below are related to the mathematics in the multiplication and division unit *How Many Packages and Groups?*. You can use the activities to enrich your child's mathematical learning experience.

Everyday Multiplication and Division Situations Think about when you use multiplication and division in your everyday life and enlist your child's help in solving these problems. Here are some examples:

○ When you plan a family reunion for 45 people, you may need forks that come in packages of 8. How many packages do you need?

○ As the coach of the school soccer team, you need to order drinks. There are 18 children on the team and 12 games during the season. Each child has 1 drink at each game. How many drinks does the school need to buy for the season? Ask your child to explain the strategies used to solve such problems.

How Did You Solve That? Encourage your child to explain his or her strategies for multiplying and dividing numbers. Students will be encouraged to develop more than one way to solve a problem and to use methods that are based on understanding numbers and their relationships. Some of these methods may not be the ones you learned in school, but you may recognize some of them as methods you use in your daily life. One of the most important things you can do is to show genuine interest in the ways your child solves problems, even if they are different from your own.

Solving 2-Digit Multiplication Problems

First, write a story to go with each problem. Then, solve the problem and show your solution. You may use arrays or pictures if they help show your strategy more clearly.

 1   53 × 24 = _____

Story problem:

Solution:

Solving 2-Digit Multiplication Problems

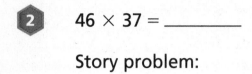 $46 \times 37 = $ _____

Story problem:

Solution:

Multiplying Two Ways

1 Solve this problem in two different ways. Be sure to show how you got your answer.

31 × 27 = _____

First way:

Second way:

Ongoing Review

2 What is the closest estimate of 39 × 22?

Ⓐ 400 Ⓑ 600 Ⓒ 800 Ⓓ 1,000

NOTE

Students solve the same 2-digit multiplication problem in two different ways.

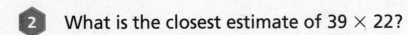 **Strategies for Solving Multiplication Problems**

NAME _____ DATE _____

Solving a Multiplication Problem

First, write a story problem for 22 × 34. Then, solve the problem and show how you solved it. You may include arrays or pictures of groups.

22 × 34 = _____

Story problem:

Here's how I solved it:

NOTE

Students use multiplication strategies that include breaking a problem apart to make smaller problems that are easier to multiply.
MWI Strategies for Solving Multiplication Problems

UNIT 7 | **446** | SESSION 1.4   © Pearson Education 4

NAME   DATE

Two Cluster Problems

Solve the first three problems in each cluster. Show your strategy for solving the final problem. Put a star next to any of the problems in the cluster that helped you.

Set A

Solve these problems:

$4 \times 3 =$

$50 \times 3 =$

$54 \times 10 =$

Now solve $54 \times 13 =$

Set B

Solve these problems:

$2 \times 38 =$

$4 \times 38 =$

$40 \times 38 =$

Now solve $42 \times 38 =$

NAME   DATE

Comparing Fractions

Fill in $<$, $>$, or $=$ to make each comparison true.

1. $\dfrac{3}{4}\ \square\ \dfrac{4}{5}$

2. $\dfrac{7}{12}\ \square\ \dfrac{1}{2}$

3. $1\dfrac{2}{3}\ \square\ 2\dfrac{1}{3}$

4. $\dfrac{5}{1}\ \square\ \dfrac{1}{5}$

5. $\dfrac{2}{12}\ \square\ \dfrac{1}{6}$

6. $\dfrac{2}{5}\ \square\ \dfrac{4}{6}$

7. $\dfrac{9}{12}\ \square\ \dfrac{7}{4}$

8. $\dfrac{0}{3}\ \square\ \dfrac{0}{8}$

NOTE

Students compare the values of different fractions.
MWI Fractional Parts

Multiplication Cluster Problems

Solve the first three problems in each cluster. Show how you solved the final problem. Put a star next to any of the problems in the cluster that helped you.

Set A

Solve these problems:

$6 \times 30 =$

$3 \times 30 =$

$30 \times 30 =$

Now solve $36 \times 33 =$

Set B

Solve these problems:

$7 \times 25 =$

$20 \times 25 =$

$40 \times 25 =$

Now solve $47 \times 25 =$

Set C

Solve these problems:

$3 \times 5 =$

$3 \times 60 =$

$40 \times 60 =$

Now solve $43 \times 65 =$

Multiplication Cluster Problems

Set D

Solve these problems:

$2 \times 57 =$

$4 \times 57 =$

$40 \times 57 =$

Now solve $44 \times 57 =$

Set E

Solve these problems:

$6 \times 25 =$

$60 \times 6 =$

$60 \times 20 =$

Now solve $64 \times 26 =$

Set F

Solve these problems:

$10 \times 45 =$

$9 \times 45 =$

$4 \times 45 =$

Now solve $94 \times 45 =$

Pencil Problems

Read each of the story problems below and answer each part of the problem. Show your solutions.

1   Lakeside School has 500 students. The principal orders 22 boxes of pencils. Each box has 24 pencils. Will he have enough pencils to give one to each student in the school?

     a. Write an estimate and explain your thinking.

     b. How many pencils are there in 22 boxes?

     c. How many more or less than 500 is that?

Pencil Problems

2 The Park City Children's Museum needs 1,000 pencils for its store. The museum orders pencils in boxes of 48. Will there be enough pencils if the museum orders 25 boxes?

a. Write an estimate and explain your thinking.

b. How many pencils are there in 25 boxes?

c. How many more or less than 1,000 is that?

NAME   DATE

Equivalent Fractions

Write each fraction below in the appropriate box. All fractions in each box must be equal.

$\frac{2}{12}$ $\frac{2}{8}$ $\frac{2}{4}$ $\frac{4}{12}$ $\frac{3}{6}$ $\frac{3}{12}$

$\frac{5}{10}$ $\frac{9}{12}$ $\frac{4}{6}$ $\frac{2}{6}$ $\frac{8}{12}$ $\frac{6}{8}$

$\frac{1}{2}$	$\frac{1}{3}$
$\frac{1}{4}$	$\frac{2}{3}$
$\frac{3}{4}$	$\frac{1}{6}$

NOTE

Students identify equivalent fractions.

MWI **Generating Equivalent Fractions**

NAME   DATE

Multiplication Story Problem

1 The school cafeteria serves 700 students during lunch. The disposable trays come in boxes of 36. Will there be enough trays if there are 21 boxes of trays?

a. Write an estimate and explain your thinking.

b. How many trays are in 21 boxes?
Show your solution.

c. How many more or less than 700 is that?

Ongoing Review

2 Which number is **NOT** a factor of 810?

   Ⓐ 405   Ⓑ 27   Ⓒ 25   Ⓓ 3

NOTE

Students make an estimate and solve a multiplication story problem.
MWI Strategies for Solving Multiplication Problems

NAME   DATE

Problems about Oranges

Solve each story problem. Show your solution. You may include arrays or pictures of groups.

1   The Sunshine Fruit Company sells oranges in boxes that hold 72 oranges. Ms. Green ordered 35 boxes for her grocery store. How many oranges does Ms. Green have to sell?

2   A fruit stand worker sells bags of oranges. There are 18 oranges in each bag. Over the weekend, the fruit stand worker sold 74 bags. How many oranges did he sell?

NOTE

Students practice multiplying 2-digit numbers by 2-digit numbers.
MWI Strategies for Solving Multiplication Problems

Making an Easier Problem

1 Solve these two problems and show your strategy.

    a. $15 \times 29 =$ **b.** $38 \times 16 =$

2 Read the story below and compare it to the problems above. How would you finish Sabrina's and Yuki's strategies?

The fourth-grade students are selling oranges to raise money for charity. The oranges come in two sizes of boxes. The large boxes contain 29 oranges each. The small boxes contain 16 oranges each.

    a. Sabrina counts up how many large boxes the class sold and counts 15 boxes. To find out how many oranges there are in total in the large boxes, Sabrina first multiplies 15 and 30. What does Sabrina have to do to finish the problem? Write down your solution, using Sabrina's first step.

    b. Yuki counts up how many small boxes the class sold and counts 38 boxes. Like Sabrina, he starts with an easier problem, multiplying 40 and 16. What does Yuki have to do to find how many oranges there are in total in the 38 small boxes? Write down your solution, using Yuki's first step.

NAME

DATE

Related Problems

Solve each set of problems below. Show your solution for the last problem in each set.

1
$7 \times 30 =$
$7 \times 29 =$

This is how I solved 7×29:

2
$20 \times 25 =$
$18 \times 25 =$

This is how I solved 18×25:

3
$3 \times 50 =$
$30 \times 50 =$
$30 \times 49 =$

This is how I solved 30×49:

4
$6 \times 22 =$
$60 \times 22 =$
$59 \times 22 =$

This is how I solved 59×22:

NAME   DATE

Solving Measurement Problems

Solve each problem and show your work.

1 A canned ham has a weight of 2 pounds. What is the weight, in ounces, of 7 canned hams? (1 pound = 16 ounces)

2 Mrs. Corelli worked in her garden for 45 minutes each day for 2 weeks. How many minutes did Mrs. Corelli work in her garden altogether over the two weeks? (1 week = 7 days)

3 How many 5-minute cartoons can be shown in one hour? (The cartoons are shown one at a time.)

4 Enrique used 12 quarts of orange juice and 17 quarts of apple juice to make fruit punch for a school picnic. How many cups of juice are in the punch? (1 quart = 4 cups)

5 One fish bowl holds 5 liters of water. How many milliliters of water would 6 fish bowls hold? (1 liter = 1,000 milliliters)

NOTE

Students use the four operations to solve problems involving measurements.
MWI **Converting Measurement**

NAME   DATE

More Related Problems

Solve each pair of problems below. Show your solution for the second problem in each pair.

1 $14 \times 20 =$ This is how I solved 14×19:

      $14 \times 19 =$

2 $30 \times 25 =$ This is how I solved 28×25:

      $28 \times 25 =$

3 $35 \times 30 =$ This is how I solved 35×29:

      $35 \times 29 =$

4 $50 \times 40 =$ This is how I solved 50×38:

      $50 \times 38 =$

NOTE

Students practice solving problems in which one factor is 1 or 2 away from a multiple of 10. Sometimes it is helpful to solve problems like these by changing that factor to a nearby multiple of 10 and adjusting the answer.

MWI Multiplication Cluster Problems

More Multiplication Cluster Problems

In Sets A–D, solve the first five problems in each cluster. Show how you solved the final problem. Put a star next to any of the problems in the cluster that helped you.

Set A

Solve these problems:

$30 \times 50 =$

$7 \times 50 =$

$37 \times 2 =$

$3 \times 52 =$

$30 \times 52 =$

Now solve $37 \times 52 =$

Set B

Solve these problems:

$6 \times 6 =$

$60 \times 60 =$

$60 \times 63 =$

$63 \times 60 =$

$3 \times 63 =$

Now solve $63 \times 63 =$

More Multiplication Cluster Problems

Set C

Solve these problems:

$50 \times 90 =$

$60 \times 90 =$

$9 \times 90 =$

$59 \times 90 =$

$59 \times 3 =$

Now solve $59 \times 93 =$

Set D

Solve these problems:

$8 \times 25 =$

$8 \times 26 =$

$80 \times 26 =$

$85 \times 10 =$

$85 \times 20 =$

Now solve $85 \times 26 =$

More Multiplication Cluster Problems

Estimate the answer to each problem. Make up a cluster of problems to help you solve each problem. Exchange clusters with a partner and solve each other's clusters.

 1    $39 \times 75 =$ Estimate: _____

 2    $44 \times 28 =$ Estimate: _____

More Multiplication Cluster Problems

Estimate the answer to each problem. Make up a cluster of problems to help you solve each problem. Exchange clusters with a partner and solve each other's clusters.

 3 $64 \times 73 =$ Estimate: _____

 4 $58 \times 46 =$ Estimate: _____

NAME   DATE

More Problems about Oranges

Solve each story problem below. Show your solutions. You may also show your solutions with arrays or pictures of groups.

1   Annie has filled her delivery truck with 70 boxes of oranges. Each box contains 50 oranges. When she gets to the supermarket, the grocer wants only 68 boxes. She decides to take the extra boxes to the food bank.

    a. How many oranges did Annie start with on the truck?

    b. How many oranges does the grocer want?

    c. How many oranges will Annie give the food bank?

2   Jim is packing oranges into boxes that are meant to hold 50 oranges. But the oranges are too big! He can only fit 49 oranges into each box. He has 36 boxes to fill. How many oranges will he need?

NAME _____   DATE _____

How Many Waffles?

Solve each problem. Use pictures and words to show how you solved each problem.

1 Three people each get $1\frac{3}{4}$ waffles. How many waffles are there in all? Draw a picture and tell how many.

_____ waffles in all

2 Draw a picture to show how four people could each have $2\frac{1}{3}$ waffles. How many waffles are there in all?

_____ waffles in all

NOTE

Students find the total amount given the number of fractional parts.
MWI Adding and Subtracting Mixed Numbers

NAME   DATE   (PAGE 1 OF 2)

Multiplying 4-Digit Numbers by 1-Digit Numbers

Solve each problem and show your work.

1 1,548 students attend Sunset Elementary School. The principal wants to make sure each student gets 5 pencils to start the school year. How many pencils does she need to buy?

2 The Fresh Fruit Company can fit 2,650 oranges in one truck. One day they sent out 3 trucks full of oranges to deliver the fruit to grocery stores. How many oranges did they send out that day?

3 $2,124 \times 4 =$

4 $3,670 \times 9 =$

Multiplying 4-Digit Numbers by 1-Digit Numbers

Solve each problem and show your work.

5 The Susan School serves 1,406 lunches per week. The Lincoln School serves 3 times as many lunches. How many lunches does the Lincoln School serve?

6 Seven truck drivers each drove 4,215 miles in a two-week period. How many miles did they drive in all?

7 $8,437 \times 2 =$

8 $4,750 \times 8 =$

NAME _____ DATE _____

Solving Another Multiplication Problem

Write a story problem for 65 × 35. Then solve the problem and show how you solved it.

 1   65 × 35 = _____

Story problem:

Here is how I solved it:

Ongoing Review

 2   Which number is **NOT** a factor of 750?

Ⓐ 250   Ⓑ 75   Ⓒ 15   Ⓓ 7

NOTE

Students solve a 2-digit-by-2-digit multiplication problem.
MWI **Strategies for Solving Multiplication Problems**

NAME _____   DATE _____

Division Practice

Solve each division problem below. Then write a related multiplication fact.

Division Problem	Multiplication Fact
1 63 ÷ 7 = _____	_____ × _____ = _____
2 72 ÷ 9 = _____	_____ × _____ = _____
3 56 ÷ 8 = _____	_____ × _____ = _____
4 64 ÷ 8 = _____	_____ × _____ = _____
5 27 ÷ 3 = _____	_____ × _____ = _____
6 49 ÷ 7 = _____	_____ × _____ = _____
7 48 ÷ 6 = _____	_____ × _____ = _____
8 36 ÷ 4 = _____	_____ × _____ = _____
9 6)42 = _____	_____ × _____ = _____
10 9)54 = _____	_____ × _____ = _____

NOTE

Students review division problems that are related to known multiplication facts.
MWI **Division and Multiplication**

Writing Multiplication Story Problems

Write a story problem for each problem. For one of the problems, write a multiplicative comparison problem. Solve each problem and show your solution.

1 $28 \times 53 =$ _____

Story problem:

Solution:

2 $3{,}573 \times 6 =$ _____

Story problem:

Solution:

Writing Multiplication Story Problems

3 $6,355 \times 8 = $ _____

Story problem:

Solution:

4 $67 \times 46 = $ _____

Story problem:

Solution:

NAME   DATE

Driving Long Distances

Ms. Ortega drives her truck to different cities from her home in Dallas, Texas. The table shows the round-trip distance to each city she travels to and how many times she made the trip last year. For each city in the table, show the total number of miles Ms. Ortega drove.

Use the space below the table to show your work.

City	Round-trip Distances	Number of Trips	Total Number of Miles
Lincoln, NE	1,302	3	
Gainesville, FL	1,954	6	
Seattle, WA	4,236	8	
Sacramento, CA	3,472	5	

NOTE

Students multiply 4-digit numbers by 1-digit numbers.
MWI **Multi-Step Problems with Larger Numbers**

NAME _____ DATE _____

How Many Legs?

Solve these problems and show your work.

How many legs do …

1   4,366 children have? _____

2   2,066 spiders have? (A spider has 8 legs.) _____

3   3,219 dogs have? _____

4   1,077 three-legged stools have? _____

5   5,910 beetles have? (A beetle has 6 legs.) _____

NOTE

Students solve problems using multiplication strategies.
MWI **Strategies for Solving Multiplication Problems**

NAME _____   DATE _____

Solving Division Problems

Solve the story problems below. Write an equation for each problem and show how you solved it so that someone else reading your solution will understand your thinking.

1 Marco wants to sell his marble collection at a yard sale. He has 112 marbles. He wants to put 8 marbles in each bag. How many bags of marbles will he have?

Equation:

Solution:

2 Marco baked 96 cookies to sell at the yard sale. He wants to fill 6 cookie tins with the same number of cookies in each tin. How many cookies should he put in each tin?

Equation:

Solution:

NOTE

Students review the meaning of division problems and practice solving them.
MWI Division Situations

Problems about Teams

Solve each of the story problems and show your solutions.
You may also use a picture to explain your thinking.

1 It is field day at Riverside School. All of the fourth-grade students are outside playing games. There are 126 students. Each team has 14 students. How many teams can they make?

2 There are 112 students in third grade. How many teams of 7 can they make?

3 There are 95 students in second grade. How many teams of 5 can they make?

Problems about Teams

4 There are 154 students in sixth grade. How many teams of 11 can they make?

5 There are 132 students in first grade. How many teams of 6 can they make?

6 There are 120 students in fifth grade. How many teams of 15 can they make?

NAME   DATE

How Many Hundreds? How Many Total?

1 Here are the numbers of postcards in six collections:
174, 96, 98, 122, 113, 151

    a. About how many hundreds of postcards are
there in all? Circle the best estimate.

       400   600   800   1000

    How did you decide?

    b. Add the numbers to find the exact total number
of postcards. Use the standard algorithm.

2 Here are the costs of 4 items at the grocery store:
$1.31, $2.71, $1.97, $3.04

    a. About how much do the 4 items cost? Circle the
best estimate.

       $7.00 $8.00 $9.00 $10.00

    How did you decide?

    b. Add the numbers to find the exact cost of the
4 items. Use the standard algorithm.

NOTE

Students estimate and solve addition problems.
MWI **Place Value: Large Numbers**

NAME   DATE

Multiplication Practice

Solve each problem in two ways. Record your solutions.

1   63 × 45 = _____
First way:

Second way:

2   72 × 56 = _____
First way:

Second way:

NOTE

Students practice multiplying two 2-digit numbers. They have been working on breaking numbers apart in a variety of ways in order to solve these problems.
MWI Strategies for Solving Multiplication Problems

Marisol's Mystery Multiple Tower

This is the top part of Marisol's multiple tower:

| 240 |
| 224 |
| 208 |
| 192 |
| 176 |

1 By what number is Marisol counting?

2 How many numbers are in Marisol's tower so far?
How do you know?

3 What is Marisol's 10th multiple?

4 If Marisol adds 5 more numbers to her tower, on what number will she land?

Problems about Multiple Towers

1 This is the top part of Amelia's multiple tower.

299
276
253
230
207

a. By what number is Amelia counting?

b. What is Amelia's 10th multiple?
How do you know?

c. What will her 20th multiple be?
How do you know?

2 This is the top part of Emaan's multiple tower.

198
180
162
144
126

a. By what number is Emaan counting?

b. What is Emaan's 5th multiple?
How do you know?

c. What will his 15th multiple be?
How do you know?

Problems about Multiple Towers

3 This is the top part of Noemi's multiple tower.

360
345
330
315
300

a. By what number is Noemi counting?

b. How many numbers are in Noemi's tower?
How do you know?

c. What is her 10th multiple?
How do you know?

4 This is the top part of Nadeem's multiple tower.

651
620
589
558
527

a. By what number is Nadeem counting?

b. How many numbers are in Nadeem's tower?
How do you know?

c. What will his 25th multiple be?
How do you know?

ACTIVITY

Solving Division Problems

Solve each problem. You may want to represent the problem with pictures. Show your solutions.

1 You have 3 decks of cards with 52 cards in each deck. How many cards will each person get if the 3 decks are dealt out evenly to 6 people?

2 Cans of juice come in cases of 24. How many cases do you need in order to give one can to each of 264 students?

3 One of the lions at the Sampson Zoo has a mass of 144 kilograms. The Flemish Giant rabbit at the zoo has a mass of 4 kilograms. How many times as great is the lion's mass compared to the rabbit's mass?

Solving Division Problems

4   12)252

5   504 ÷ 6

6   11)360

NAME _____   DATE _____

City Sports Leagues

Solve each of the story problems and show your solutions.
You may also use a picture to explain your thinking.

1 126 kids have signed up for the city soccer league.
They want 9 kids on each team. How many teams can
they make?

2 138 kids have signed up for the city baseball league.
They want to make 6 teams. How many kids can they
put on each team?

3 192 kids have signed up for the city youth basketball
league. They want to make 24 teams. How many kids
can they put on each team?

NOTE

Students practice solving division problems.
MWI **Division Strategies**

Dividing 4-Digit Numbers by 1-Digit Numbers

Solve each problem and show your work.

1 In one day at Honeysweet Apple Orchard, workers picked 1,549 apples. They want to put them in bags of 6. How many bags can they fill?

2 1,004 children signed up to play in the Smith City youth basketball league. 8 children will be placed on each team. How many teams of 8 players will there be?

3 $2,831 \div 5$

4 $5,346 \div 7$

Dividing 4-Digit Numbers by 1-Digit Numbers

Solve each problem and show your work.

5   1,452 shirts were delivered to a large department store. They came in boxes with 4 shirts in each box. How many boxes were delivered?

6   3,020 letters need to be mailed out to members of the City Service Club. Five people are stuffing the envelopes. If each person stuffs the same number of envelopes, how many envelopes will each person stuff?

7   A fish tank at Sea Wonder Aquarium contains 1,876 gallons of water. It has 4 times as much water in it as the largest fish tank at Under the Sea Aquarium. How many gallons of water are in the fish tank at Under the Sea Aquarium?

8 $2,287 \div 3$

Solving a Division Story Problem

1 Ms. Kim's students have 185 books in their classroom library. She puts 45 books on each shelf.
a. How many shelves have 45 books?

b. How many books are on the last shelf?

Ongoing Review

2 What is the next multiple in this multiple tower?

Ⓐ 180   Ⓑ 189   Ⓒ 191   Ⓓ 193

162
135
108
81

NOTE

Students solve a division problem in a story context.
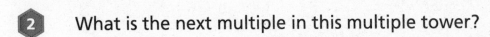 **MWI** **Remainders: What Do You Do With the Extras?**

NAME _____ DATE _____

Writing a Division Story Problem

1 Choose one of the division problems below and circle it. Write a story problem to go with it. Then solve the division problem, and show your solution. (You may do more than one problem if you have time.)

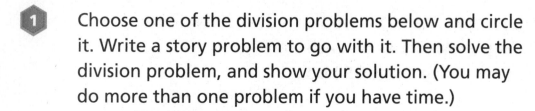

144 ÷ 8   135 ÷ 9   169 ÷ 13

Story problem:

Solution:

Ongoing Review

2 Richard had $6.47. He spent $4.28 on a poster. How much money does Richard have left?

Ⓐ $10.75   Ⓑ $2.29   Ⓒ $2.19   Ⓓ $1.19

NOTE

Students have been working on solving division problems with 2-digit and 3-digit dividends. It is often helpful to think of a division problem in a story context.

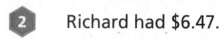 **Division Situations**

NAME   DATE

Multi-Step Problems

For each problem, write an equation with a letter to stand for the unknown. Solve the problem and show your work.

1 There are 28 cans of cranberry juice in a case. A grocery store received a shipment of 5 cases of cranberry juice. The store has sold 15 cans so far. How many cans does the store have left to sell?

2 There are 12 apples in a bag. The Santos family really likes apples and bought 8 bags. They have eaten 18 apples so far. How many apples are left?

3 The Lakeside School bought 35 boxes of pencils. Each box has 24 pencils. The students have used 600 of the pencils so far. How many pencils are left?

NAME _____   DATE _____

Multi-Step Problems

For each problem, write an equation with a letter to stand for the unknown. Solve the problem and show your work.

4 An ice cream store sold 12 pints of chocolate ice cream and 16 pints of vanilla ice cream. The store sells ice cream in 1-cup containers. How many cups of ice cream did the ice cream store sell? (1 pint = 2 cups)

5 Anna and Venetta made 2 liters of lemonade for their lemonade stand. They sold 1,500 milliliters of lemonade at the stand. Then they poured the remaining lemonade into two glasses with an equal amount of lemonade in each glass. How much lemonade did they pour into each glass? (1 liter = 1,000 milliliters)

6 Jake practiced the piano for 4 hours and 40 minutes this week. He practiced for the same amount of time each day. How many minutes did he practice each day? (Reminder: There are 7 days in a week.)

Dividing Large Numbers

Solve each problem and show your work.

1 A football stadium has 4,890 seats. There are 6 sections of seats with the same number of seats in each section. How many seats are in each section?

2 A big company is planning to have a dinner for 1,418 people. How many tables are needed if 8 people can sit at each table?

3 2,212 ÷ 7

4 4,676 ÷ 2

NOTE

Students divide 4-digit numbers by 1-digit numbers.

MWI Division Strategies

NAME   DATE

Division Problems about Pencils

Solve each problem below and show your solutions. You need these two pieces of information for these problems.
○ Pencils come in packages of 12.
○ There are 23 students in Mr. Coburn's class.

1 How many packages of pencils does Mr. Coburn have to open to give 2 pencils to every student in his class?

2 How many packages of pencils does Mr. Coburn have to open to give 4 pencils to every student in his class?

3 How many packages of pencils does Mr. Coburn have to open to give 6 pencils to every student in his class?

NOTE

Students practice understanding story problems and solving division problems.
MWI Division Situations

© Pearson Education 4

ACTIVITY

Solving Multiplication and Division Problems

For each problem below, first make a close estimate.
Then solve each problem, and show your work.

1 Cory buys stickers in packages of 36 for his sticker
collection. Last year, he bought 97 packages of stickers.
How many stickers did he buy?

Estimate:

Solution:

2 Tanya has 460 sports cards in her collection, which she
keeps in a binder that holds 8 cards on a page. How
many pages does she need?

Estimate:

Solution:

Solving Multiplication and Division Problems

3 The city soccer league has 1,273 players who have signed up to play on teams. They want to make teams of 9 players. How many teams can they form?

Estimate:

Solution:

4 The fourth-grade students sold packages of seeds to raise money for their class trip. Last week, they sold 1,130 packages of seeds. This week they sold 4 times as many packages as they sold last week. How many packages of seeds did they sell this week?

Estimate:

Solution:

NAME

DATE

Flea Market

Solve each problem and show your work.

1 Mr. Diaz makes bracelets and sells them at flea markets. He uses 8 beads for each bracelet. Mr. Diaz has a bag of 1,500 beads. How many bracelets can he make?

2 Ms. Lang has a collection of 2,106 old postcards that she bought at flea markets. She stores them in 6 boxes, with the same number in each box. How many postcards are in each box?

3 $3,241 \div 7$

4 $6,708 \div 4$

NOTE

Students divide 4-digit numbers by 1-digit numbers.
MWI Division Strategies

NAME

DATE

Selling Fruit

Solve each problem and show your work.

1 A grocery store received a shipment of 25 crates of oranges. There were 14 oranges in each crate. Over the weekend, they sold 137 oranges. How many oranges are left?

2 A grocery store got a shipment of 208 pounds of cherries. The store sells the cherries in 8-ounce bags. The store sold 15 bags of cherries. How many bags of cherries are left? (I pound = 16 ounces)

3 A grocery store sells pink grapefruit for $2.00 per pound, and ruby red grapefruit for $2.50 per pound. One day, the store sold 6 pounds of pink grapefruit and 9 pounds of ruby red grapefruit. How much money did the store receive for the grapefruits?

NOTE

Students practice solving multi-step problems.
MWI **Converting Measurement**

Penny Jars and Towers

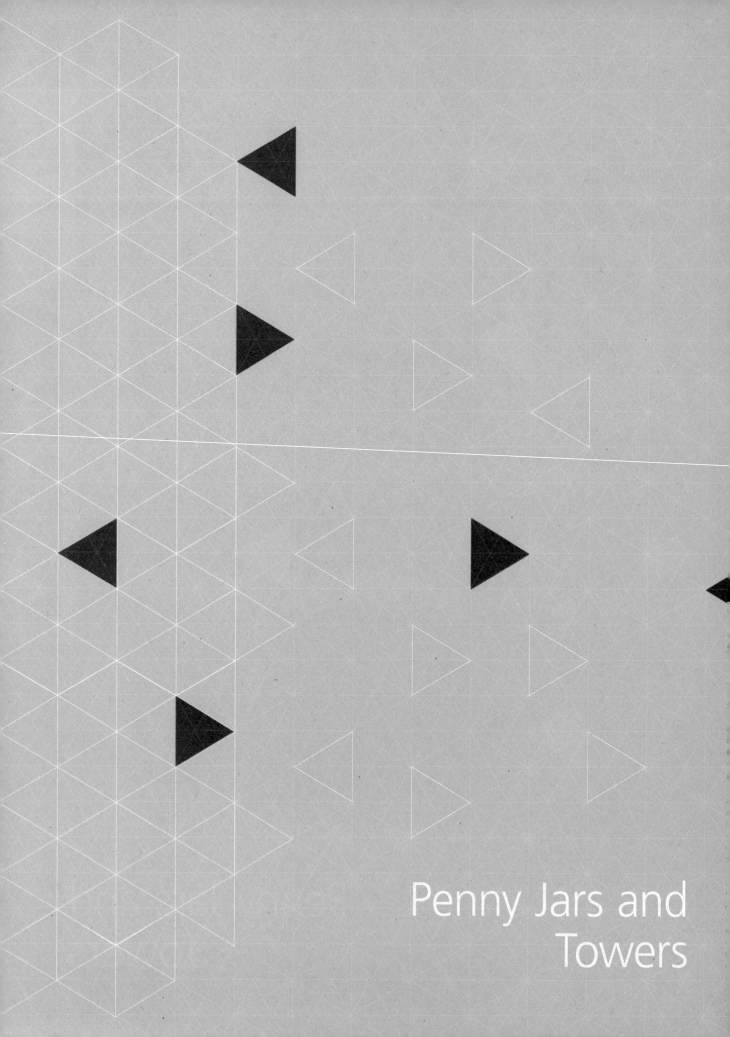

Penny Jars and
Towers

NAME _____ DATE _____

Penny Jar Amounts

1 Fill in the numbers for your first Penny Jar situation:

    a. Start with _____ pennies. Add _____ pennies each round.

    b. How many pennies are in the jar after 6 rounds?

2 Fill in the numbers for your second Penny Jar situation:

    a. Start with _____ pennies. Add _____ pennies each round.

    b. How many pennies are in the jar after 6 rounds?

Penny Jar Situations

Choose one of your Penny Jar cards. Draw a picture or a diagram that shows the number of pennies in the jar after each round. Show at least 6 rounds.

NAME   DATE

A Vegetable Farm

Solve each story problem below and show your solutions.
You may also use a picture to explain your thinking.

1   Ms. Mason is packing pumpkins into crates. She has
216 pumpkins, and each crate can hold 8 pumpkins.
How many crates does she need?

2   Mr. Lee needs to pack potatoes. He has 24 sacks to
pack 288 potatoes. How many potatoes can he put in
each sack?

3   Mr. Gorton stores corn in boxes. There are 47 boxes
with 95 ears of corn in each box. How much corn does
he store?

NOTE

Students practice solving multiplication and division problems in story problem contexts.
MWI Division Situations

NAME   DATE

Closest Estimate

Circle the closest estimate.

1 1,788 × 4 ≈	700	6,000	7,000
2 3,421 ÷ 6 ≈	500	600	700
3 2,109 × 5 ≈	10,000	12,000	100,000
4 1,770 × 8 ≈	10,000	12,000	14,000
5 5,738 ÷ 3 ≈	190	1,900	18,000
6 6,525 ÷ 9 ≈	700	800	900

NOTE

Students estimate products and quotients.
MWI Place Value: Large Numbers

NAME   DATE

About the Mathematics in This Unit

Dear Family,

Our class is starting a new mathematics unit about patterns and change called *Penny Jars and Towers*. In this unit, students learn to use tables and equations to represent various situations in which one quantity changes in relation to another quantity. They describe and compare different situations of change, and discuss the relationship between them. Throughout the unit, students will be working toward these goals:

Benchmarks/Goals	Examples
Generate a number pattern that follows a given rule and analyze features of the pattern in order to solve problems.	I started with 6 pennies in a jar. I added 4 pennies each day. Will there ever be 157 pennies in the jar?
Model the mathematics of a situation with tables and with mathematical notation, including using letters to represent unspecified quantities.	Make a table that shows how many pennies are in the jar after day 1, day 2, up to day 10. | Day	0	1	2	3	4
Number of Pennies	6	10	14	18	22	 Write an equation that shows how many pennies are in the jar on day 20.
Solve multi-step word problems using the four operations.	How many windows, including skylights, are there in a double tower with 15 floors? Skylights Windows

Please look for more information and activities about *Penny Jars and Towers* that will be sent home in the coming weeks.

Penny Jar Table

 1

a. Fill in the numbers for a Penny Jar situation:

Start with _____ pennies. Add _____ pennies each round.

b. Complete this table:

Number of Rounds	Total Number of Pennies
Start with	
1	
2	
3	
4	
5	
6	
7	
10	
15	
20	

Penny Jar Table

2 How did you determine the number of pennies after round 10?

3 How did you determine the number of pennies after round 20?

4 What is a general rule you can use to find the total number of pennies in the jar after any round?

NAME _____ DATE _____

Solving Division Problems

Solve each problem. Show your solutions.

1 352 ÷ 21

2 17)459 _____

3 Venetta has 405 pictures to put in an album. Each page of an album holds 12 pictures. How many pages does Venetta need for all of her pictures?

Ongoing Review

4 Which number is **not** a multiple of 24?

    Ⓐ 120   Ⓑ 264   Ⓒ 300   Ⓓ 360

NOTE
_____

Students practice solving division problems.
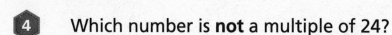 **Division Strategies**

NAME   DATE

Adding Pennies to a Penny Jar

There are 8 pennies in the jar at the start. We add 5 pennies each round. After 1 round there are 13 pennies.

1 How many pennies are in the jar after 2 rounds?

2 How many pennies are in the jar after 4 rounds?

3 How many pennies are in the jar after 6 rounds? How do you know?

4 Use a picture, diagram, or table to represent this Penny Jar situation in the space below.

NOTE

Students have been working with these Penny Jar situations in class. They use what they know about the start amount and the repeated change to figure out the total number of pennies at a future point.

MWI Penny Jar Comparisons

NAME   DATE

Related Activities to Try at Home

Dear Family,

The activity below is related to the mathematics in *Penny Jars and Towers*. You can use this activity to enrich your child's mathematical learning experience.

Marble Jar Start with 4 objects in a jar (marbles, pennies, paper clips, or some other small objects). Each day, add 6 more of the same object. Help your child record how many objects are in the jar at the end of each day. Have your child predict how the number of objects in the jar will change over the next few days. Repeat the Marble Jar activity with other numbers (e.g., start with 5 objects and add 9 each day; start with 100 objects and subtract 6 each day).

Number of days	Number of marbles
Start with	4
Day 1	10
Day 2	16
Day 3	22
etc.	

Penny Jar Patterns

1 Complete the following table for this Penny Jar situation:
Start with 6 pennies. Add 10 pennies each round.

Number of Rounds	Total Number of Pennies
Start with	
1	
2	
3	
4	
5	
6	
7	
10	

2 Write a rule for this Penny Jar situation. First write it in words. Then write it as an equation.

3 Will there ever be exactly 157 pennies in the jar after some round? Why or why not? Try to find the answer without calculating the total for every round up to 157.

Penny Jar Patterns

4 Complete the following table for this Penny Jar situation: Start with 2 pennies. Add 3 pennies each round.

Number of Rounds	Total Number of Pennies
Start with	
1	
2	
3	
4	
5	
6	
7	
10	

5 Write a rule for this Penny Jar situation. First write it in words. Then write it as an equation.

6 Will there ever be exactly 90 pennies in the jar after some round? Why or why not? Try to find the answer without calculating the total for every round up to 90.

Penny Jar Patterns

7   Complete the following table for this Penny Jar situation: Start with 3 pennies. Add 2 pennies each round.

Number of Rounds	Total Number of Pennies
Start with	
1	
2	
3	
4	
5	
6	
7	
10	

8   Write a rule for this Penny Jar situation. First write it in words. Then write it as an equation.

9   Will there ever be exactly 501 pennies in the jar after some round? Why or why not? Try to find the answer without calculating the total for every round up to 501.

NAME   DATE

Adding Pennies to a Penny Jar 2

There is 1 penny in the jar at the start. We add 4 pennies each round. After 1 round there are 5 pennies.

1   Complete this table to show what happens for 7 rounds.

Number of Rounds	Total Number of Pennies
Start with	
1	
2	
3	
4	
5	
6	
7	

2   How many pennies will be in the jar after 10 rounds? How did you figure this out?

NOTE

Students use a table to record the total number of pennies in a jar, given that the number of pennies changes at a constant rate. In class, students have been using what they know to figure out the total number of pennies in a jar after a round that is not listed in a table.

MWI A Table for a Penny Jar Problem

NAME   DATE

Solve in Two Ways, Multiplication

Solve each problem in two ways. Record your solutions.

1 $76 \times 29 =$ _____

First way:

Second way:

2 $34 \times 88 =$ _____

First way:

Second way:

NOTE

Students practice solving 2-digit multiplication problems. They work on efficiency and flexibility by solving the problem in two ways.
MWI Strategies for Solving Multiplication Problems

UNIT 8 | **517** | SESSION 1.3   © Pearson Education 4

Round 20

Here is a Penny Jar situation: Start with 5 pennies.
Add 6 pennies each round.

1 Complete this table for this Penny Jar situation.

Number of Rounds	Calculation	Total Number of Pennies
5		
10		
15		
20		

2 How did you find the amount for round 20?

Round 20

3 Jake says that the total number of pennies after round 20 is double the number after round 10 because 20 is double 10. Marisol disagrees and says that Jake's method will not work. Do you agree with Jake or with Marisol? Why?

a. Write your explanation in words.

b. Create a representation for this Penny Jar situation that shows your ideas about whether doubling works.

NAME _____ DATE _____

How Many Windows? How Many Cars?

Solve each problem below. Show your work.

1 There are 625 windows on Steve's apartment building. Each floor of the building has the same number of windows. If the building is 25 stories tall, how many windows are on each floor?

2 The office building next to Steve's apartment is 77 stories tall. If there are 44 windows on each floor, how many windows are there in all?

Ongoing Review

3 When the parking garage is completely full, it holds 900 cars. There are 12 levels in the garage. Each level holds the same number of cars. How many cars can be parked on each level?

Ⓐ 15   Ⓑ 20   Ⓒ 25   Ⓓ 75

NOTE

Students practice solving multiplication and division problems.
MWI Division Situations

Penny Jar Tables

Here are the tables for two Penny Jar situations. Complete the tables and then show how you figured out the answers to the questions.

Table A

Number of Rounds	Total Number of Pennies
Start with	7
1	11
2	
3	
4	23
5	27
6	
7	

1 How many pennies are there after 10 rounds? _____

2 How many pennies are there after 20 rounds? _____

NOTE
_____

Students use patterns in tables to fill in missing values for two Penny Jar situations and determine the total number of pennies for later rounds.
MWI **Rules to Describe Penny Jar Situations**

Penny Jar Tables

Table B

Number of Rounds	Total Number of Pennies
Start with	6
1	
2	16
3	
4	26
5	
6	36
7	

3   How many pennies are there after 10 rounds? _____

4   How many pennies are there after 20 rounds? _____

NAME   DATE

Penny Jar Tables A and B

Round	Penny Jar Situation A: Total Number of Pennies	Penny Jar Situation B: Total Number of Pennies
Starts with	1	12
1	4	14
2	7	16
3	10	18
4	13	20
5	16	22
6	19	24
7	22	26
10		
15		
20		

NAME

DATE

Estimate and Solve

Make an estimate for each problem. Then solve the problem.
Show your solution.

1 $53 \times 71 =$

Estimate: _____

Solve:

2 $18 \times 93 =$

Estimate: _____

Solve:

3 $45 \times 55 =$

Estimate: _____

Solve:

Ongoing Review

4 What is the closest estimate for $420 \div 15$?

Ⓐ 20 Ⓑ 30 Ⓒ 40 Ⓓ 42

NOTE

Students estimate the product of two numbers and then find the actual product.

MWI Strategies for Solving Multiplication Problems

NAME _____   DATE _____

Your Own Penny Jar

Make up a Penny Jar situation.

1 Start with: _____

Add each round: _____

2 Complete this table:

Number of Rounds	Total Number of Pennies
Start with	
1	
2	
3	
4	
5	
10	
15	
20	

3 Write an arithmetic expression for how many pennies will be in the jar after 100 rounds.

NOTE

Students complete a table and use the pattern in it to find a value that occurs later in the table.
MWI The Penny Jar

ACTIVITY

Windows and Towers

1 Fill in the table for the single tower.

Single Tower

Number of Floors	Number of Windows
1	
2	
3	
4	
5	
6	
7	
8	
9	
10	

2 a. How did you figure out the number of windows on 10 floors?

b. Write an arithmetic expression that shows how you figured this out.

3 a. How many windows are there on 15 floors?

b. Write an arithmetic expression that shows how you figured this out.

Windows and Towers

4 Fill in the table for the double tower.

Double Tower

Number of Floors	Number of Windows
1	
2	
3	
4	
5	
6	
7	
8	
9	
10	

5 **a.** How did you figure out the number of windows on 10 floors?

b. Write an arithmetic expression that shows how you figured this out.

6 **a.** How many windows are there on 15 floors?

b. Write an arithmetic expression that shows how you figured this out.

NAME _____ DATE _____

Solve in Two Ways

Solve each problem in two ways. Show your solutions.

1 $741 \div 19 =$ _____

First way:

Second way:

2 $66 \times 34 =$ _____

First way:

Second way:

Ongoing Review

3 What is the closest estimate of 38×43?

Ⓐ 120   Ⓑ 160   Ⓒ 1,200   Ⓓ 1,600

NOTE

Students solve multiplication and division problems in two ways.

MWI Strategies for Solving Multiplication Problems

NAME

DATE

Solving Multiplication Problems

Solve each problem and show your work.

1 $49 \times 25 =$ _____

2 $60 \times 76 =$ _____

3
```
    32
  × 43
```

4
```
    78
  × 45
```

NOTE

Students multiply two 2-digit numbers.

MWI **Strategies for Solving Multiplication Problems**

Giant Penny Jars

Solve the problems and show your solutions.

1 A Giant Penny Jar starts with no pennies in the jar.
It gets filled with 6 pennies each day for 3 years.
(Each year has 365 days.)

   a. How many pennies are in the jar after 3 years?

   b. At the end of 3 years, how much money is in the jar
   in dollars and cents?

Giant Penny Jars

2 At Market Street School, students have collected 3,153 pennies at the rate of 5 pennies each day. There were some pennies in the jar at the start.

a. For how many days have the students collected pennies?

b. How many pennies were in the jar when they started?

Giant Penny Jars

3 A Giant Penny Jar had 600 pennies in it at the start. People put 125 pennies in the jar each day.

a. Make a table that shows how many pennies are in the jar for each of the first 8 days.

b. On day 12, will the number of pennies in the jar be odd or even? How do you know? Find the answer without calculating the number of pennies in the jar for that day.

Giant Penny Jars

c. On day 25, will the number of pennies in the jar be odd or even? How do you know? Find the answer without calculating the number of pennies in the jar for that day.

d. On which days in your table is the total number of pennies a multiple of 100?

e. What are the next three days that will have a total number of pennies that is a multiple of 100? How do you know?

Square and Corner Towers

Fill in the tables and answer the questions.

Square Tower

Number of Floors	Number of Windows
1	
2	
3	
4	
5	
6	
7	
8	
9	
10	

1   **a.** How did you figure out the number of windows on a tower with 10 floors?

     b. Write an arithmetic expression that shows how you figured this out.

2   **a.** How many windows are there on a tower with 100 floors?

     b. Write an arithmetic expression that shows how you figured this out.

Square and Corner Towers

Corner Tower

Number of Floors	Number of Windows
1	
2	
3	
4	
5	
6	
7	
8	
9	
10	

3 **a.** How did you figure out the number of windows on a tower with 10 floors?

  b. Write an arithmetic expression that shows how you figured this out.

4 **a.** How many windows are there on 100 floors?

  b. Write an arithmetic expression that shows how you figured this out.

© Pearson Education 4

NAME _____ DATE _____

Pizza Problems

Solve each story problem and show your solutions. You may also use a picture to explain your thinking.

1 There are 11 people at a pizza party. Each person wants 3 slices of pizza, and each pizza has 8 slices. How many pizzas should they order?

2 At a larger pizza party, there are 18 people. Each person wants 3 slices, and each pizza has 8 slices. How many pizzas should they order?

3 At a smaller pizza party, there are 7 people. They order 3 pizzas. Each person eats 3 slices, and each pizza has 8 slices. How much extra pizza do they have?

NOTE

Students practice solving multi-step story problems involving multiplication and division.
MWI Remainders: What Do You Do With the Extras?

NAME   DATE

Writing Multiplication Story Problems

For each problem, write a story problem. Then solve the problem and show your solution.

 1   **82 × 39 = _____**

Story problem:

Solution:

 2   **56 × 91 = _____**

Story problem:

Solution:

NOTE

Students practice solving 2-digit multiplication problems.
MWI **Strategies for Solving Multiplication Problems**

Backward Problems for Single and Double Towers

Single Towers

Can a single tower ever have exactly this many windows?
Circle Yes or No. If yes, write how many floors the tower has.

1 60 windows?

Yes   No

2 61 windows?

Yes   No

3 62 windows?

Yes   No

4 63 windows?

Yes   No

5 64 windows?

Yes   No

6 65 windows?

Yes   No

7 Can a single tower have exactly 105 windows?
Explain your answer.

Backward Problems for Single and Double Towers

Double Towers

Can a double tower ever have exactly this many windows?
Circle Yes or No. If yes, write how many floors the tower has.

8 80 windows?

Yes   No

9 81 windows?

Yes   No

10 82 windows?

Yes   No

11 83 windows?

Yes   No

12 84 windows?

Yes   No

13 85 windows?

Yes   No

14 Can a double tower have exactly 108 windows?
Explain your answer.

Backward Problems for Square and Corner Towers

Square Towers

Can a square tower ever have exactly this many windows?
Circle Yes or No. If yes, write how many floors the tower has.

1   90 windows?

Yes   No

2   91 windows?

Yes   No

3   92 windows?

Yes   No

4   93 windows?

Yes   No

5   94 windows?

Yes   No

6   95 windows?

Yes   No

7   Can a square tower have exactly 135 windows?
Explain your answer.

Backward Problems for Square and Corner Towers

Corner Towers

Can a corner tower ever have exactly this many windows?
Circle Yes or No. If yes, write how many floors the tower has.

8 90 windows?

Yes   No

9 91 windows?

Yes   No

10 92 windows?

Yes   No

11 93 windows?

Yes   No

12 94 windows?

Yes   No

13 95 windows?

Yes   No

14 Can a corner tower have exactly 123 windows?
Explain your answer.

NAME   DATE

Benson's Mystery Multiple Tower

The picture shows part of Benson's multiple tower.

1 What number is Benson counting by?

594
567
540
513
486

2 How many numbers are in Benson's tower so far? How do you know?

3 If Benson adds five more numbers to his tower, what number will he land on?

Ongoing Review

4 What is the 15th multiple in Benson's tower?

Ⓐ 15   Ⓑ 275   Ⓒ 405   Ⓓ 450

NOTE

Students find factors and multiples using a multiple tower.
MWI Multiple Towers

NAME   DATE

A Table and a Rule

Here is a Penny Jar situation: Start with 26 pennies.
Add 4 pennies each round.

1 Complete the table shown below.

Number of Rounds	Total Number of Pennies
Start with	
1	
2	
3	
4	
5	
6	
7	
8	

2 How many pennies will be in the jar after 30 rounds?

3 Write a rule for the total number of pennies in the jar
after any round.

NOTE

Students complete a table and interpret the patterns that are found in the table. They also
make general rules for finding the total number of pennies in the Penny Jar after any round.
MWI Rules to Describe Penny Jar Situations

Rules for Towers: Singles and Doubles

1 For a **single** tower, how would you find the number of windows

    a. if there are 20 floors?

    b. if there are 30 floors?

    c. if there are 45 floors?

2 Write a rule for finding the number of windows on a single tower for any number of floors. You can use words or numbers and letters.

3 For a **double** tower, how would you find the number of windows

    a. if there are 20 floors?

    b. if there are 30 floors?

    c. if there are 45 floors?

4 Write a rule for finding the number of windows on a double tower for any number of floors. You can use words or numbers and letters.

Rules for Towers: Corners and Squares

1 For a **corner** tower, how would you find the number of windows

    a. if there are 20 floors?

    b. if there are 30 floors?

    c. if there are 45 floors?

2 Write a rule for finding the number of windows on a corner tower for any number of floors. You can use words or numbers and letters.

3 For a **square** tower, how would you find the number of windows

    a. if there are 20 floors?

    b. if there are 30 floors?

    c. if there are 45 floors?

4 Write a rule for finding the number of windows on a square tower for any number of floors. You can use words or numbers and letters.

NAME   DATE

Summer Reading

Solve each story problem and show your solutions.

1 Tonya has a new 364-page book to read when she goes on vacation. She is going on vacation for 14 days, and she wants to read the same number of pages each day. How many pages will she read each day?

2 Derek signed up for a summer reading challenge. He wants to read 75 pages every day in July. There are 31 days in July. How many pages will he read in July?

3 Cheyenne plans to read 35 pages every day in July and 40 pages every day in August. There are 31 days in August, too.

   a. How many pages will Cheyenne read in July?

   b. How many pages will Cheyenne read in August?

NOTE

Students practice solving multiplication and division problems in real-world contexts.
MWI Division and Multiplication

Penny Jar Problems

1 Complete the table for the following Penny Jar situation: Start with 2 pennies. Add 4 pennies each round.

Number of Rounds	Total Number of Pennies
Start with	
1	
2	
3	
4	
5	

2 Will there ever be exactly 50 pennies in the Penny Jar after a certain round? If so, after what round? How do you know?

3 Will there ever be exactly 51 pennies in the Penny Jar after a certain round? If so, after what round? How do you know?

NOTE

Students use tables to help them think about the relationship between two quantities.
MWI A Table for a Penny Jar Problem

© Pearson Education 4

Penny Jar Problems

4 Which of these will never be the total number of pennies in the jar after a certain round: 52, 53, or 54?

5 Choose one number of pennies that you know will be the total number of pennies in the Penny Jar after a certain round. Explain how you know.

6 Choose one number of pennies that you know can never be the total number of pennies in the Penny Jar after a certain round. Explain how you know.

Saving Money

Steve earns $0.50 each day for feeding his family's dog and making his bed. He wants to save $10.00 to buy some trading cards. He starts with $3.00.

1 Complete the following table.

Number of Days	Amount Saved
Start	$3.00
1	
2	
3	
4	
5	
10	
15	

2 How many days will it take him to earn enough money if he does his chores every day and saves what he earns?

3 Write an arithmetic expression to show how much money he will have saved after 30 days.

NOTE

Students solve real-world problems involving the math content of this unit.
MWI Multi-Step Problems With Larger Numbers

© Pearson Education 4

NAME _____   DATE _____

Removing Pennies from a Penny Jar

Here is a Penny Jar situation: Start with 95 pennies.
Remove 4 pennies each round.

1 Make a table to show what happens for 8 rounds.

Number of Rounds	Total Number of Pennies
Start with	
1	
2	
3	
4	
5	
6	
7	
8	

2 When will there be 0 pennies in the jar? Show how you figured this out.

NOTE

Students use what they know about the starting number of pennies in the penny jar and the change in the number of pennies during each round to figure out the total number of pennies in a later round.

MWI A Table for a Penny Jar Problem